Population, Resources & Environment

2014-2015 Revised Printing

George F. Clark

Rutgers University

www.kendallhunt.com
Send all inquiries to:
4050 Westmark Drive
Dubuque, IA 52004-1840

ISBN 978-1-4652-5656-0

Printed in the United States of America

Introduction

I have been associated with this course for over 30 years – first as the Teaching Assistant for Gretchen Condran, then for Bill Mosher when he was here as her one-year replacement, and since then as its Instructor. When I first worked with the course, it was deemed an "Area A" or "mission" course, and it was primarily an issues course. Students read disparate opinions on population-related issues, learned a bit about population basics, and we showed a childbirth film because most students had not seen a birth. Our students did a couple of short papers, and took two or three exams. We had large enrollments, some students taking the course to fulfill an area requirement, others out of interest, and many for a combination of both reasons.

Then the University went through reorganization, Cook College's requirements changed, and "*PRE*" lost its role as an "Area A" course. It still, however, fulfills the Cook (now "SEBS") diversity requirement. It is required for majors in the Department of Human Ecology and is an optional course for our minor as well. The course has evolved and changed in other ways, too.

When I first taught "*PRE*", we had a second, more "nuts and bolts" population course – "*Introduction to Population Studies*". As "*PRE*" lost much of its broader role in the College, and as the Department dropped "*Population Studies*", the two were merged into the modern version of "*PRE*" – in the direct sense, a "nuts and bolts" course, in the indirect sense, an issues course. We will discuss many population-related issues along the way, but not just and not primarily the ones we covered in the old "*PRE*" – food, resources, pollution, economic development, and so on. In fact, population's influence is far more pervasive and subtle than just those topics – we are all affected by it in ways most people haven't considered.

Thus, we will begin with consideration of how population affects us – how who we are (demographically) and when we were born influences our lives. Then, we'll cover three "themes" – the Basic Demographic (or, Population Component) Equation, the range of population perspectives, and the "POET" scheme for analyzing population's role in the world today. We'll do a thumbnail sketch of the population past, present, and potential futures, followed by what I like to call "The Dreaded Data Lecture" – the sources from which we obtain population data. I call it that because for most students it's a less than fascinating topic. We'll cover population composition next – population characteristics, ascribed and achieved.

The middle of the semester will be taken up by looking at the individual components of population change in some depth – mortality, fertility, and migration. For each of these, we'll examine sources of data, coverage and content errors, measures, patterns and trends, differentials (how who we are affects things such as our chances of reaching a ripe old age, how many children we have, and how likely it is that we'll move) and "points to ponder" about each. At the end of the course we'll return to our themes in greater depth, look at how the various perspectives on population see its role in the traditional issues, and conclude with policy options.

There are three other points to make. First, of necessity, studying population involves numbers. I do not (with only a few exceptions) expect you to memorize numbers or to do complicated calculations. I *do* expect you to understand the strengths and weaknesses of different measures, to understand when it's appropriate to use which measures, and to understand what they mean. There is really nothing here for the non-quantitatively inclined to worry about – very few students have significant problems in this regard.

Second, I am most concerned with teaching you *how* to think about population matters – to give you the tools to do so in a more sophisticated manner; I am *not* concerned with *what* you think or to teach you what I think. I have been told by many of my former students how useful "*PRE*" was to them in ways they did not anticipate – both in other courses and on the job. The basics of population are a useful tool in a variety of ways; media coverage of population is often inexact and sometimes flat-out wrong, the same is sometimes true of academics in professional articles, and often someone is trying to make an argument based on misinterpreted or incompletely interpreted population data. You should be able to see through that and to question it. When I took my first population course as an elective at Rutgers in 1970, I *thought* that I knew the role of population…my own views continue to evolve as new trends and arguments and evidence emerge. Experts disagree on population issues, so there's no reason why I should pretend to be teaching you demographic "truth and beauty". You'll have the tools and exposure to the perspectives – what you make of them is up to you.

Third, I'd like to discuss the origin of this book. In the old days we used a "reader" – a book that had representative articles giving the Neomalthusian, Moderate, Marxist and/or High Tech views on each population issue. When the course changed I used a couple of different texts – neither exactly what I wanted for the course. Every semester my students would respond in a similar fashion – about a third hated the text, found it useless, and resented the expense, another third or so loved the text and found it worthwhile, and the final third was rather neutral. For the next few years I relied on handouts, and with the exception of a few students each semester, most wee satisfied – although a common complaint/suggestion was that they should be offered in bound form so that they would be easier to keep together and would be something that could last. I can still place a text on reserve for those who need or desire one, but this format has seemed to be successful for everyone involved – Kendall-Hunt, me, and, most importantly, you the students. I make no money from this book – royalties go to the Department of Human Ecology for the benefit of our students – just for the record. This version includes a little more material and some more recent data where available. I hope that you will find it useful and enjoyable.

Population continues to be important and dynamic – and thus an ever-fascinating topic. Recently, for example, New Jersey has given a great deal of attention given to sprawl. Sprawl is the result of migration patterns – and dealing with it is no easy task. It has major consequences for all of us in terms of transportation (e.g., congestion and environmental impacts – Route 18 and Route 1), planning facilities for the future (e.g., schools or dormitory space at the University), socially (e.g., residential segregation by age, social class, etc.), and politically (e.g., the state versus municipalities). This is but one small example. Hardly a week goes by without a significant population-related story or two in the news. Individually, locally, regionally, nationally, and globally, population's impacts are numerous, diverse, and crucial. If you leave the course with an appreciation for and an understanding of this fact, we should be content.

So, welcome to "*PRE*". I hope you learn a lot, think a good deal, perhaps appreciate how fortunate we all are as compared to most of the world, and have some fun along the way.

George F. Clark
June, 2014

Approximate Schedule for the Semester

Week #1: Introduction & Why Population Is Important

Week #2: Population "Themes" & Population Past

Week #3: Population Present & Future

Week #4: Sources of Population Data & Population Composition

Week #5: Population Composition

Week #6: Mortality

Week #7: Mortality

Week #8: Mortality/Fertility

Week #9: Fertility

Week #10: Fertility

Week #11: Migration, Immigration, & Urbanization

Week #12: Migration, Immigration, & Urbanization

Week #13: Return To Themes & Population Issues

Week #14: Population Issues

Week #15: Population Policy & Wrap-Up

You'll notice that there are no examination dates. That's because we'll decide early on how many exams there will be, and then we'll schedule them as go along so as to maximize convenience for as many members of the class as possible. In a class of this size, there will never be a date upon which everyone can agree; if this applies to you at some point, feel free to negotiate an alternative time with me. There will be an exam during the finals period.

In all honesty, I should also note that I rarely end up sticking to the above schedule (or any schedule, for that matter) precisely. Sometimes we go faster than I anticipate; more often we fall behind due to a cancelled class or extended discussion on a particular topic – hence the term "approximate" above. I'll keep you informed as we proceed.

Population "Themes"

Much of what we'll be doing this semester revolves around the deceptively simple – so it seems – Basic Demographic Equation, also known as the Population Component Equation. In its long form, it looks like this:

Population $_{\text{Time 2}}$ = Population $_{\text{Time 1}}$ + Births – Deaths + Inmigration – Outmigration

Times 1 and 2 generally refer to one year (they can be thought of as starting population and final population, respectively). Births, deaths, in-movement and out-movement are the only ways in which a population can change. For countries, states, counties, towns, et cetera, all four factors must be considered. We can re-group the components, however, as:

Population $_{\text{Time 2}}$ = Population $_{\text{Time 1}}$ + (Births – Deaths) + (Inmigration – Outmigration)

The difference between births and deaths is called natural increase (or decrease, where deaths exceed births); the difference between inmigration and outmigration is called net migration (which can be positive or negative). At the *world* level, we don't have to worry about net migration, so the equation becomes:

Population $_{\text{Time 2}}$ = Population $_{\text{Time 1}}$ + Births – Deaths

Thus, at the world level, all population growth comes from the difference between births and deaths – natural increase (and perhaps someday, natural decrease). In turn, this means that we only have three choices for reducing population growth – decrease fertility, increase mortality, or a combination of the two. As most of us would be reluctant to advocate increasing mortality, we are really left with only one choice – reducing fertility. Then, the question becomes *how*.

To take a more local example, we can examine New Jersey's components of population change from July 1, 2011 to July 1, 2012 from the U.S. Census Bureau:

8,864,590 = 8,834,773 + (102,379 births – 69,686 deaths) + (46,609 immigrants from abroad – 49,465 net migrants to other states). Thus:

8,864,590 = 8,834,773 + (32,673 from natural increase) + (-2,856 from net out-migration).

Beyond the fact that New Jersey added an estimated 29,817 people between 2011 and 2012, who was added is just as important – there is a qualitative as well as a quantitative aspect to population change. The loss of New Jersey's residents in terms of internal migration was more than offset by the gain from international migration in numbers and natural increase. Further, those who came here from abroad are obviously different from those who left for other states. The latter group mostly was not foreign born, was likely more affluent, better educated, and probably consisted disproportionately of students leaving to attend college out of state, retirees, and similarly specific groups. The overall result is the increasing diversification of New Jersey ethnically, racially, and so on. So the Population Component Equation can reflect both quantitative and qualitative change. For the U.S. as a whole, we grew by about 2,326,224 between 2011-12, gaining 885,804 from legal immigration and 1,440,420 from natural increase (3,953,593 births and 2,513,173 deaths).

A second theme is the spectrum of population perspectives in terms of population's role in world problems. They can be envisioned as lying along a line:

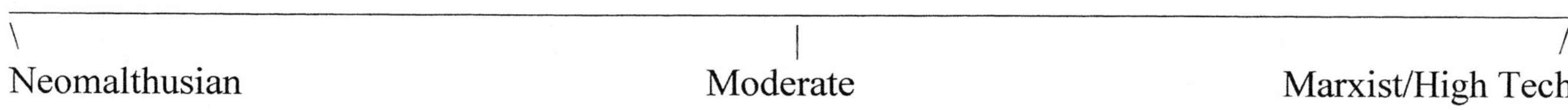

For Neomalthusians, population is ***the*** problem – the fundamental factor underlying all others. For Moderates, population is ***a*** problem – a crucial factor in world problems, but one of many. Marxists and High Techs are grouped together at the other end because they come to a similar conclusion about the role of population, but for different reasons. For Marxists, population is a ***false*** problem – it is used as a smokescreen issues by those with money and power to obscure what they see as being the "real" problem – one of economic and social disparity. High Techs see population as ***no*** problem – indeed, for many of them population is actually a plus because it spurs us on to new discoveries and inventions – in other words, "progress". We'll return to these later in the semester. Not conveniently fitting on the spectrum, but worthy of mention nonetheless, is what might be termed the "Deep Ecology" viewpoint. These are people who argue that the environment should come first; they are anti-population like the Neomalthusians, but not from the same vantage point.

The third theme is the "POET" scheme, so named for its four components – Population, Organization (in the social and economic sense), Environment, and Technology. POET is useful in analyzing population-related issues and in illustrating the causal scheme the population perspectives employ. The general form (identical to the purely Moderate view as well) appears below.

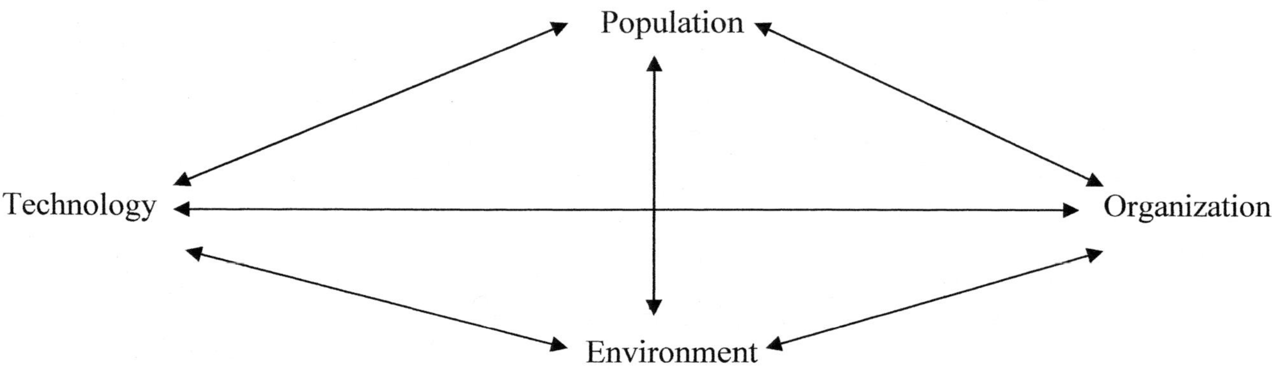

Each component affects and is affected by each of the others. We can show how the other perspectives see the world, too. Below is the Neomalthusian perspective – population is the independent variable or causal factor, and the others are the dependent variables or effects.

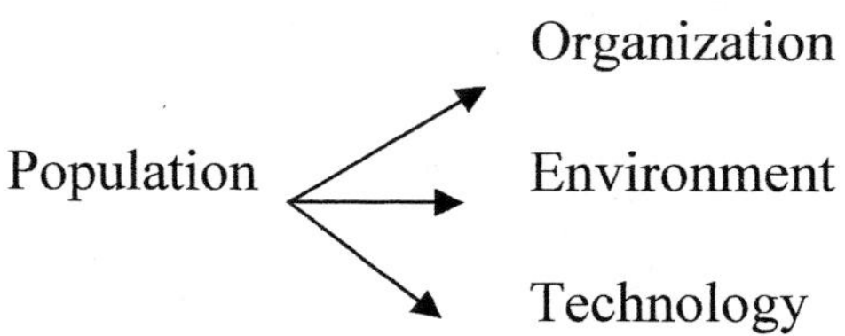

Marxist – organization is the independent variable, the others are the dependent variables.

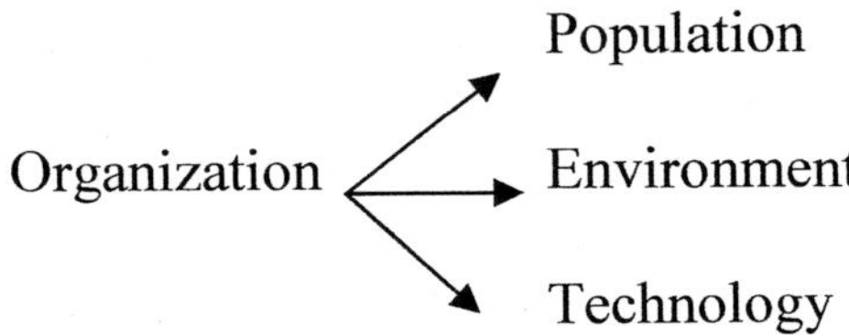

High Tech – technology is the independent variable, the others are the dependent variables.

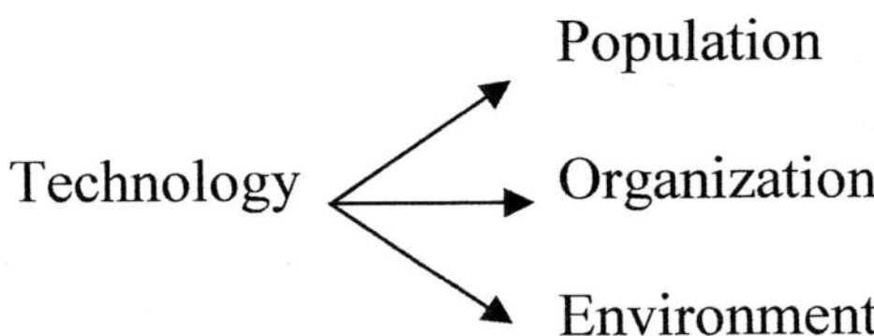

While the others illustrate how each perspective thinks the world works, for the Deep Ecology or Green perspective, it's more a matter of how the world *should* work, according to them:

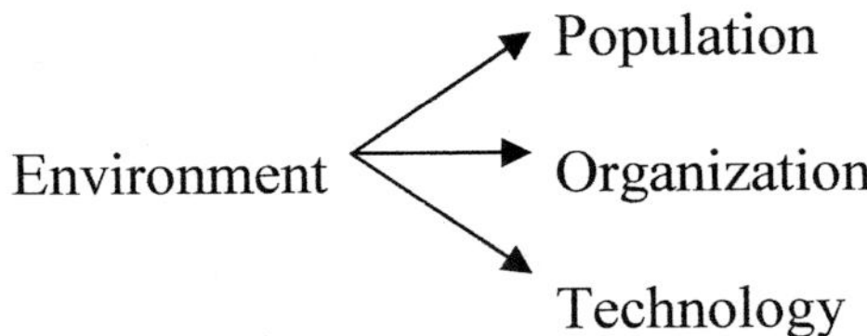

You can and should keep these three themes in kind as we go through the semester. When we return to the major issues at the end of the course, you don't have to "buy" any particular one of these views, and you might find that you think population is crucial to resource depletion, but technology is vital to pollution, and organization to economic development. Again, there is no agreement about population's role even among experts – if there were, this course would be very different and presumably the world would be, too. Thus, you're entitled to your informed opinion. Whether you come back to population in your studies, work, or just as a concerned citizen of the world, you should reevaluate your opinions in light of new information…almost 40 years after taking my undergraduate population course, I realize how much less I knew then than I thought I did at the time – and I'm still learning.

Population Past

For the vast bulk of human history, population growth was negligible and would have been unnoticed by hunter-gatherer societies. One of the most popular population "myths" is that there are more people alive today than in the rest of human history combined – *not* true. Historical demographers estimate that somewhere between 70 and 100 billion people have lived – far more than our current 6+ billion. It took all of human history until 25,000 years ago for the world population to reach something like the current population of Chicago – about 3 million. Even 2,000 years ago, world population was probably comparable to the U.S. population today – somewhere around 200-300 million. At that point, life expectancy was likely ~20, the Rate of Natural Increase was ~ .0005%, and doubling time was about 1,500 years

Observers differ slightly, but we hit the 1 billion mark ~1800 or shortly thereafter. After taking 99.9%+ of human history to reach that milestone, it only took about another 130 years to achieve the 2nd billion, only 30 years to hit the 3rd, and a mere 15 to make the 4 billion mark. We added the 5th and 6th billions in about 12 years each. These billions came faster even though the rate of natural increase has been declining for the last 25-30 years. Why? Because the base population grew ever-larger. Demographers think – and most hope – that future billions will come more slowly from here on out. If you look at the data described above, imagine what could happen if the historical pattern *didn't* change. Can you envision 12 billion on the planet by mid-century?

If that sounds impossible for you to imagine, consider my own life experience. When I was born in 1949, world population was less than 2.5 billion, the U.S. population was about 150 million, and New Jersey had 4.9 million people. When I started as an undergraduate at Rutgers, world population was about 3.5 billion, the U.S. population was still less than 200 million, and New Jersey had less than 7 million people. In June of 2009 the Census Bureau's "Population Clocks" estimate world population at about 6.7 billion and the U.S. population at 306 million. As we saw earlier, New Jersey's population is more than 8.8 million. Thus, in my lifetime the world population has more than doubled, the U.S. population has doubled, and New Jersey's population has increased by more than 75%. I'm not ***so*** old to have seen so much change. Imagine if we see equivalent change in ***your*** lifetime! For those of you born in 1988, so far you've seen New Jersey's population grow from 7.7 to 8.8 million, the U.S. population from 246 million to 309 million, and the world population from 5.1 billion to 6.8 billion – and ***you*** definitely aren't that old! World population should hit the 7 billion mark in 2012 or thereabouts.

Billion	Date	Doubling Time
1	1800	
2	1930	130 years to go from 1 to 2 billion
3	1960	
4	1975	45 years to go from 2 to 4 billion
5	1987	
6	1999	39 years to go from 3 to 6 billion
7	2012	

At the time of the first U.S. Census in 1790, we had less than 4 million people. Virginia was the largest state at almost 700,000, and New Jersey had 184,000 people. Philadelphia and New York City were no larger than present-day New Brunswick. By 1900, the country had 76 million people, New York was the largest state at more than 7.2 million, and New York City had almost 3.5 million. Today, California has 36.5 million and New York City has approximately 8.2 million people.

Population Present

According to the Population Reference Bureau's *2013 World Population Data Sheet*, world population in mid-2013 was estimated at 7.137 billion. As we have been adding approximately 80 million people per year recently, that means we are heading for the 8.0 billion mark in the 2020s. 1.2 billion are found in MDCs (More Developed Countries), 5.9 billion in LDCs (Less Developed Countries). With more than 90% of growth occurring in LDCs, their share of the world population continues to rise. From this source, here are some key characteristics of the world, MDCs, LDCs, and world regions (not synonymous with continents, in the traditional sense).

Place	Population	CBR/CDR/RNI			Doubling Time	Density
World	7.137 billion	20	8	1.2%	58 years	52
MDCs	1.246 billion	11	10	0.1%	350 years	27
LDCs	5.891 billion	22	7	1.4%	50 years	71
Africa	1.100 billion	37	11	2.6%	27 years	36
North America	352 million	12	8	0.4%	175 years	16
Latin America & The Caribbean	606 million	19	6	1.3%	54 years	30
Oceania	38 million	18	7	1.1%	64 years	4
Asia	4.302 billion	18	7	1.1%	64 years	135
Europe	740 million	11	11	0.0%	(700+ years)	32

In class, we'll discuss this and more further. For now, the CBR = Crude Birth Rate, CDR = Crude Death Rate, RNI = Rate of Natural Increase, and Density = # people per square kilometer.

According to the United Nations, MDCS include all of Europe and North America, Australia, Japan and New Zealand; all other countries are considered LDCs. The United Nations also has a special category of Least Developed Countries – a sub-set of LDCs that are the worst off countries in the world. 40 countries are considered "least developed", almost all of them in Africa.

You may notice several points of interest in the table above. For example, Asia has more than half of the world's population and is the world region with the highest density. Africa is usually seen as the world's most problematic area in terms of population, yet it is not very densely populated. That's because density doesn't tell us much about resources available – such as water and arable land for example. This reflects the limited value of simple population density, a point we'll look at more closely later in the semester. You might notice that Europe has natural decrease. This implies that we can look at its "halving time" instead of its doubling time. What else in the table strikes you as important or interesting or perhaps surprising?

Beyond the table above, 90% of the world's population lives on 10% of the land. The majority of the world population is in the northern hemisphere, and much of it is found along coastal areas and hence at low altitudes. The world is rapidly urbanizing –for the first time, about half of the world population lives in an urban area, and that proportion continues to grow. Of course, "urban" worldwide is generally defined as places of 2,000 or more, so maybe that's not quite as impressive as it seems at first glance. However, 21% of the world's population lives in cities of 750,000 or more, and that, too, will continue to grow.

In class we'll also look at the world's largest countries and the largest and smallest states in the United States. How many of these do you think you can name? We'll see how well the class can do collectively.

Population Future - Projections

Population projections (***NOT*** "predictions") make assumptions about the components of population change; the projections are population figures resulting from these assumptions. The Census Bureau does series of projections – low, middle and high – and then numerous variations within each. The actual population size for the projected date should fall between the extremes, and presumably closest to the middle series. Using an example in class, however, you'll see that this doesn't always happen. Shorter-term projections usually are more accurate than longer ones, but sometimes that isn't true, either. Doubling time is a "projection" only in the sense that it does assume that whatever is happening now will continue to happen indefinitely; it's not really a "true" projection. Below are projections data and the assumptions made for two points in the future for the United States – 2050 and 2100. These were taken from the Census Bureau's web site. See what you think about them and which assumptions and projections you think will be most on target.

Assumptions 1999->2100	Total Fertility Rate # Children/Woman	Life Expectancy at Birth in Years, Male/Female	Annual(Legal) Immigration in Thousands
Low Series:	2.0358->1.6321	74.0/79.7->85.0/89.3	739->117
Middle Series:	2.0475->2.1829	74.1/79.8->88.0/92.3	954->926
High Series:	2.0592->2.7374	74.1/79.8->92.3/95.2	1,191->3,039

The population of the United States this year is approximately 311 million; here are the projections for 2050 and 2100 based on the three sets of assumptions. Also included is the "zero immigration" series of projections. It uses the fertility and mortality assumptions of the middle series, but further assumes **no** net immigration. This projection is not made because zero immigration seems a realistic possibility, but rather to illustrate the direct and indirect effects of immigration. "Direct" means the addition of the immigrants themselves; "indirect" means the additional contribution of their children and grandchildren. If you compare the middle series and the zero immigration series, you can see that immigration is expected to add approximately 76 million more people by 2050 and 193 million by 2100 above that added by natural increase.

Series	2050	2100
Low	313,546,000	282,706,000
Middle	403,687,000	570,954,000
High	552,757,000	1,182,390,000
Zero Immigration	327,641,000	377,444,000

The Census Bureau's 2008 projection for 2050 is 439 million; it assumes birth rates will be ~2.0 children per woman, slowly rising life expectancy, and rising (legal) immigration. In the year 2050 it projects that we'll have 5.653 million births, 4.249 million deaths, and 2.047 legal immigrants. Thus, we would gain 1.403 million people via natural increase, but almost 60% of our population growth would be from immigration, a much higher proportion than today. Our population growth rate would fall from .98% to .79%.

Next is population composition. Our population will grow and change in composition. There's been a lot of publicity about whites becoming a minority in the U.S. in this century...that depends on the definitions of race. For most purposes, the Census Bureau includes data on Hispanics *with* other racial groups, yet they are included *under* the other racial groups as well. In other words, they are not considered a distinct race, but rather to be of Hispanic Origin and classified under one of the other headings. Hispanic Origin people are counted twice – in a sense. Hispanic Origin is thus a unique category – not a racial group like the others, but more than an ethnic group. However unsatisfactory this may be, no alternative has yet to be agreed upon. Look at "Ascribed Characteristics" to see differing interpretations of our future in racial breakdown.

The "Demographic Transition Model", Population Growth Curve, & Population Size Graph

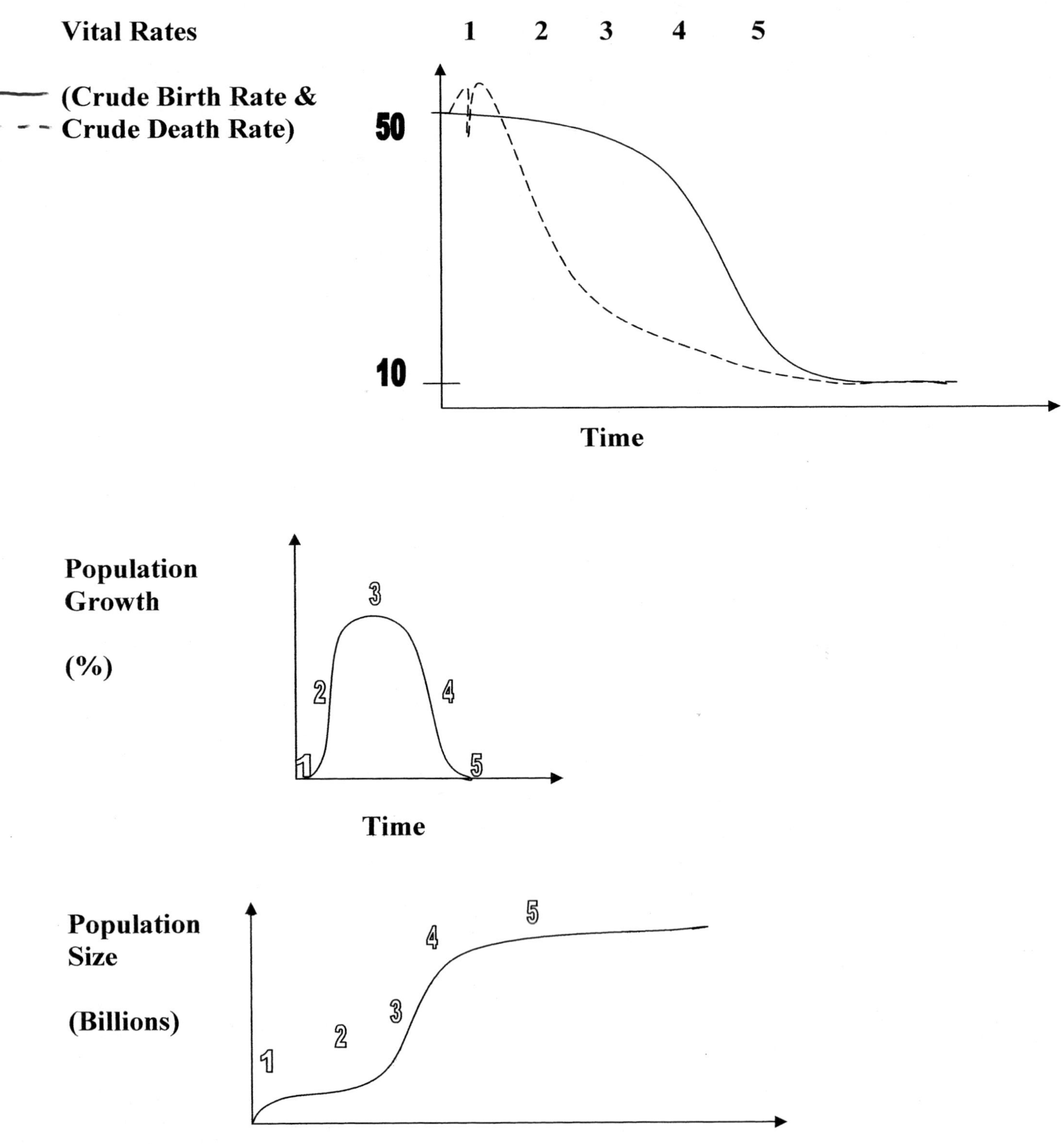

The preceding graphs reflect what used to be called the "Demographic Transition Theory". It was an attempt to use the experience of MDCs to explain and to predict how populations go from the conditions that prevailed for most of human history – high, fluctuating death rates, high birth rates, and near-zero population growth – to conditions of low death rates, low, fluctuating birth rates, and near-zero population growth. What was called the "theory" of this transition is now downgraded to a "model" because the more recent experience of LDCs has been much more variable than the experience of MDCs.

The first graph shows five stages of the transition as follows:

Stage	CBR	CDR	RNI
1	high	high and fluctuating	~0
2	high	declining	increasing
3	high	low	peak
4	declining	low	decreasing
5	low	low	~0

The dotted line represents death rates and the solid line represents birth rates. I prefer a 5-stage version of the model; others use 3-stage or 4-stage versions. The gap between the birth rate line and the death rate line at any point in time is the rate of natural increase per 1,000 population. For example, at peak growth, the CBR might be ~50 per thousand, the CDR ~10 per 1,000 population. So the rate of natural increase would be 40 per 1,000 population, or 4.0%. The model is ***highly*** idealized; the actual experience of individual MDCs was not so "neat" or clear.

The second graph is derived from the first and shows how the RNI changes over time throughout the transition. This is key because we can locate countries or regions on the model and then anticipate what's likely to happen to them in the future. MDCs are in late Stage 4 or Stage 5 – their population growth is about over in most cases. The United States, Canada and Australia are exceptions to this because there all receive significant amounts of immigration. LDCs range from mid-Stage 2 to Stage 4. If – and it's a big "if" – those in Stage 2 follow the model, it means that their peak population growth is yet to come. It *is* possible that they will have a different pattern – some seem to – so that birth and death rates may decline together from here on out. It's also possible that some are "stuck" in Stage 2 or Stage 3 – or may even regress unless we find a preventative and/or a cure for HIV/AIDS.

The third graph is also derived from the first and shows what happens to size as a population goes through the transition. Thus, even though the population begins and ends with near-zero growth, the period in between produces much larger populations at the end. The world as a whole has a CBR = 21 and a CDR of 9; that would put it in late Stage 4. The RNI has been decreasing, and demographers expect it to continue to do so – but we don't know how long it will take to get to Stage 5. The longer it takes, the higher the ultimate population size before the world population stabilizes and perhaps eventually starts to decline. The same is true for countries – the longer an LDC stays in Stages 2-4, the larger its population will be – a time penalty of sorts.

The situation of LDCs today is very different than the circumstances MDCs were in when they were going through the transition. For example, technology is much more sophisticated today compared to 100-200 years ago, the population is much larger, some resources may have been depleted – and others created, and MDCs were "more" developed then, relatively speaking, while LDCs are "less" developed today. LDCs can import knowledge and technology generally and specifically related to fertility and mortality – contraception, vaccines, and so on. You can think about how you see the future of LDCs in light of the model and of the differences in circumstances. Since the LDCs make up the bulk of the world population, they will determine the population future of the world as a whole in large measure. You should also make sure you understand how the three graphs are interrelated. Flawed as it is, the Demographic Transition Model does give us a way of viewing our past, where we are today, and our future.

The world today has a CBR of 20 and a CDR of 8, putting it in late stage 4. For those who are concerned with population, that's the good news – most demographers believe that the end of population growth is in sight, and zero growth will be reached within the next century. The bad news is how many more people will be added be when that occurs – likely another 2 billion or more.

Sources of Population Data

There are four main sources of population data – the census, vital registration, surveys, and miscellaneous/historical data. Each has its unique strengths and weaknesses, and each has its uses. Taken together, they comprise the data with which demographers work.

There are also two types of errors in the data sources – errors of coverage and errors of content (sometimes called errors of classification). The first refers to who's missed – or, over-counted. The second refers to bad data – incorrect information. I'll go over both the sources of data and the error types with greater specificity in class, but following are some basic points.

Most people are familiar with the census – at least the Census of Population and Housing conducted by the United States Bureau of the Census every 10 years, in years ending in 0. The census gives us counts – compositional data on key characteristics. These counts are also important in calculating birth and death rates and other measures. Coverage is imperfect – not surprising in a country headed for 300 million people. Content can be problematic as well – people can lie, sometimes an individual feels a given set of choices does not offer one that accurately describes him or her, and so on.

Our census has been mandated by the Constitution for Congressional redistricting and has been used for that purpose since 1790; it has also come to be used to allocate federal monies (approximately 400 billion dollars) on a per capita basis. Our census is *de jure*, meaning that people are counted where they usually reside. Some countries do a census that's *de facto* – people are counted wherever they happen to be on census day. Our official census day is April 1 of years ending in 0 – some say it's an appropriate date to use, because the census creates so much controversy. Unbeknownst to most people, the Census Bureau takes a variety of other censuses every five years (on a 2 & 7 or 4 & 9 cycle), including the censuses of wholesale and retail trade, construction, mining, selected services, education, agriculture, transportation and governments. In 2010, the census changed dramatically – it was shortened a great deal and was one of the shortest versions in many decades. Previously, there was a short version most people received and a long version that about 1 in 6 households received that contained many more specific population and housing questions. The traditional questions have been subsumed into The American Community Survey, which is an ongoing look at America that uses a sophisticated sampling procedure. Since the census is only constitutionally mandated for reapportionment, the ACS fulfills the need for other data at less expense. In the 2000 census, the long form had 53 questions, including such items as marital status, education, birthplace, language, previous residence, occupation, earnings and income, military experience, and physical, mental or emotional conditions. Housing questions included type and age of residence, rooms, value (or rent), taxes, fuels used, plumbing and kitchen facilities, and cars.

In class I'll show you a copy of the 2010 Census form; it had only ten questions:

1. The number of people living in the residence.
2. Whether there were additional people there on April 1 who were not included in the first question..
3. Whether the residence was a house, apartment or mobile home.
4. The person's name.
5. The telephone number.
6. Sex.
7. Age on April 1, 2010 and date of birth.
8. Whether the person was of Spanish/Hispanic/Latino origin and if so, specific background.
9. Race, including combinations and self-designation.
10. Whether there are people in the household who sometimes live somewhere else.

Questions 4, 6, 7, 8, 9 and 10 were asked for each individual in the household, as well as that person's relationship to the person filling out the form. The other questions were at the household level and only had to be answered once. Even in this age of high speed computers, the Census Bureau will still be releasing data from the 2010 Census until 2013 – it's a very time-consuming task. At the same time, they'll begin planning for the 2020 census

In the United States we register births, deaths, marriages, and divorces. Unlike many other MDCs, we do not register internal migration. This is the source for most of our information concerning fertility and mortality. Coverage is quite good – almost all of us have had our births registered and almost all of us will have our deaths registered as well. Content is a bit less certain. For example, cause of death is often complicated and an individual may have several medical conditions that potentially could be listed as the cause of death. Or, sometimes, as a kindness to survivors, a suicide will be listed as an accidental death. We also have a registration system of sorts that covers *legal* immigration; given the amount of political and media attention paid to illegal immigrants, it clearly leaves much to be desired in terms of coverage and content, too. In class I'll show you examples of the forms used to register births and deaths – you might be surprised at some of the details involved.

Surveys are used to fill in data gaps, to get at things we can't try to find out about any other way, to look at controversial topics, and to gauge people's intentions. By definition, surveys don't strive for total coverage; they're as good as their sampling procedures and response rates allow. With respect to content, I'm sure you've heard the expression "garbage in, garbage out", and that about sums it up. Surveys are used to find out contraceptive practices, childbearing intentions, migration preferences and intentions, and so forth. They are sometimes used in LDCs where a census and/or registration system are nonexistent, erratic, or of poor quality. Some surveys are an ongoing part of federal data gathering, some are by academics interested in particular phenomena, and some are privately done. As noted earlier, many of the questions that were previously included in the census are now part of The American Community Survey, one of the largest ongoing efforts by the federal government.

Historical/miscellaneous data is the final source and is something of a residual category. Once we go back in time, we don't have to back very far before data through the other three sources is unavailable. Obviously, surveys can only be done in the present, our registration system only became complete in the 1930s, and although the census goes back to 1790, for much of its existence what it had to offer was very limited. So, to do historical work, demographers use whatever they can find – cemeteries, family bibles and church records, newspapers, city directories, anything at all that might shed light on their topic. I'll show you an example of a city directory for Bangor, Maine when I was living there during graduate school in the 1970s; New Brunswick and many other communities had them for many years. While they varied in the amount of information they provided, they did offer a clue about population change over time. In the present, miscellaneous sources such as car registration and driver's license applications, school records, moving van companies, and similar sources can give us a clue about demographic shifts in population distribution, for example. Federal tax records would be useful to demographers, but are not available to them. In both historical and contemporary cases, coverage and content are dubious – but that's all demographers have available to them.

Put together, there are often still topics we'd like to know more about but which have relatively little information compiled and accessible to the researcher. Until recently, the census had grown; now it's slowly shrinking in length and questions are being dropped. Where we once talked about doing a "mini-census" in years ending in 5, now some are suggesting that we do a national survey instead of a census. Private enterprise is making more and more use of demographic data, yet the federal government has talked about scaling data collection back – ironically, in this – the "information age". For a time, there was talk of selling most census data instead of making it freely available as has traditionally been the case; the age of the internet seemed to change that, as well as protests from academics.

On the worldwide level, the data for many LDCs are quite poor. Population data is not a priority for them – understandably so. In many LDCs, taking a census is an irregular event and one that is not of high quality in terms of content or coverage. The same is true for their registration systems. Often we forced to rely on surveys and miscellaneous sources in those cases. Since most population growth is occurring in LDCs, it is ironic that we have the least and lowest quality data for the very places that are most important demographically. Where we will go from here will be interesting in the years ahead when it comes to population data, both in the United States and worldwide.

Population Composition

Population composition refers to characteristics – *who* a people are in terms of such attributes as age, sex, marital status, and education. Many students seem to confuse population composition and population distribution – which we'll look at later and which refers to *where* people are. After all these years of teaching this course, I still have no explanation for this confusion.

Who we are as the individuals who comprise a population matter to what the German social scientist Max Weber called *life chances* – our prospects for health, wealth, and longevity. There are two types of characteristics – ascribed and achieved. Ascribed characteristics are those we are born with and into, and which are difficult – if not impossible – to change. These include age, sex, race, and ethnicity. Achieved characteristics are those we can choose or change – religion, marital status, education, occupation, and income.

Social scientists use these to study and to predict behaviors and attitudes. These appear on virtually all surveys, whether done by academics or by marketing firms, for that reason. Informally, when we meet new people, we ask about many of these or take them in as best we can, because we identify each other along these lines. These are important to demographers too, for they influence our probability of reaching a ripe old age, how many children we have, and how likely we are to move or to immigrate. In the sections on mortality, fertility, and migration we'll use these as differentials – how who we are affects our demographically-related behaviors.

We'll look at achieved characteristics first, then at ascribed characteristics. Of all of these, age and sex are the two most important factors in looking at a population's future. A young population has the possibility and even likelihood of continued population growth – its age structure gives it growth momentum. An old population is unlikely to experience much, if any, population growth. Some would also see sociological implications, in that an old population might be seen as "stagnant" and a young one "dynamic". Or, a heavily male population might be seen as more aggressive and a female one more passive – based on traditional stereotypes. Some of the data that follows might surprise you, and you can see where you fit into the greater scheme of things in our society.

After the two pages of data is an estimated age-sex population pyramid for the United States as of 1/1/10. Population pyramids are "snapshots" of a population's age and sex structure at one point in time. From a pyramid we can deduce where the population might be headed demographically and perhaps something about where it has been with regard to mortality and fertility. We can also correlate significant historical events to particular age-sex groups that were the most affected by them. For example, men born in the late 1910s and early 1920s were those most directly affected by World War II, while several different age-sex groups were influenced by the Great Depression. The Great Depression reduced immigration, kept mortality higher than it would have been otherwise, and kept fertility lower. Fertility is usually the greatest single determinant of a pyramid's shape; at the least, it sets the parameters of each birth cohort because it can never increase in size, except via immigration. Under circumstances such as war or long-term in- or out-migration, mortality and migration can have visible effects, too. For example, wars can cause a "dent" in young adult males on the pyramid. Or, places with a lot of outmigration often have something of a "figure 8" shape, as those most likely to leave are young adults. These are usually found at local levels and are exceptional cases. At the level of countries, fertility is usually the single largest factor in determining a population pyramid's shape.

There are four characteristic pyramid shapes – "regular triangle", "expansive", "constrictive", and "near-stationary" – each associated with particular stages of the demographic transition model. The "regular triangle" is characteristic of a Stage I country with high and roughly equal fertility and mortality, and with near-0 population growth. An "expansive" pyramid indicates a Stage II – mid-Stage III population, with high fertility, declining or low mortality, and increasing or peak population growth. "Constrictive" pyramids indicate a population with decreasing population growth from falling fertility and low mortality – late Stage III and Stage IV. Finally, a "near-stationary" type is typical of Stage V – low and roughly equal fertility and mortality and near-0 population growth. These will be illustrated and discussed in class. Meanwhile, what can you see in the U.S. population pyramid?

Population Composition – Achieved Characteristics

Marital Status (% adults aged 18+)

Status	1920	1965	2010
Never Married	36.9	17.7	26.2
Married	57.6	76.2	56.5
Widowed	4.6	3.7	6.2
Divorced	0.6	1.9	10.3

Religion (based on 2002-8 survey data)

Religious Group	%	Specific Groups	%
Total Christian	76.0	Catholic	25.1
Total Other	3.9	Baptist	15.8
Athiest	0.7	Muslim	0.6
Agnostic	0.9	Hindu	0.4
No Religion	13.3	Jewish	1.2
Refused Reply	5.2	Buddhist	0.5

Over the last 20 years, the % belonging to a congregation has ranged from 65-71% and the % who attended in the previous 7 days from 38-44%.

Education (%s for adults aged 25+)

Level	1940	1960	2012
≤ eighth grade	60.4	39.6	5.0
some high school	15.2	19.2	7.3
high school	14.3	24.6	30.4
some college	5.5	8.8	26.3 (includes 9.6% with two-year degrees)
≥ college	4.6	7.7	30.9 (19.8% with bachelor's. 11.1% with an advanced degree)
median	8.6	10.4	13.0+ (median education figure is an estimate)

Occupation (2011 % breakdown)

Category	%	Trend	Examples
Manager/Professional Specialty	36.0	declining	lawyers, teachers, dentists
Service Occupations	18.3	rising	police, cooks, maids
Sales & Office Occupations	24.5	rising	cashiers, real estate agents
Natural Resources/Construction	9.1	declining	mechanics, farmers, loggers
Production/Transportation	12.1	rising	bakers, bus drivers

Income (2012, households)

Level	%
<$15,000	13.0
$15,000-$24,999	11.7
$25,000-$34,999	10.7
$35,000-$49,999	13.6
$50,000-$74,999	17.5
$75,000-$99,999	11.7
≥$100,000	21.8

Median: $51,107
Mean: $71,274

% Distribution by Fifths(2011)
% of total national income

Fifth	1970	2011
Lowest Fifth	5.4	3.2
Second Fifth	12.2	8.4
Middle Fifth	17.6	14.3
Fourth Fifth	23.8	23.0
Highest Fifth	40.9	51.1
(top 5%	15.6	22.3)

In 1960, 22.2% of the U.S. population was below the poverty level, in 2011 15.0% were. In 1960, 14.9% of American children were below the poverty level and 24.6% of the elderly; the comparable percentages for 2011 were 21.9% and 8.7%, with 13.7% of those 18-64 below the poverty line (the 2011 poverty threshold for an individual was $11,702, for a family of 2 it was $15,063, for a family of 3 it was $17,595, for a family of 4 it was $23,201, and for a family of five it was $27,979).

Data above is taken from: U.S. Bureau of the Census, *Statistical Abstract of the United States: 2000*(120th edition.) Washington, D.C., 2000 published by Hoover's Business Press, the *2002 Statistical Abstract* (122nd edition) published by the U.S. Census Bureau, Washington, D.C. 2002, the *2003 Statistical Abstract* (123rd edition) published by the U.S. Census Bureau, Washington, D.C. 2003, the *2006 Statistical Abstract* (126th edition) published by the U. S. Census Bureau, Washington, D.C. 2005 the *2008 Statistical Abstract of the United States* (128th edition) published by the U.S. Census Bureau, Washington, D.C. 2007, the *2010 Statistical Abstract of the United States* (130th edition) published by the U.S. Census Bureau, Washington, D.C. 2009 and the *2012 Statistical Abstract f the United States* (132nd edition) published by the U.S. Census Bureau, Washington, D.C., 2010.. Earlier editions were also consulted for this page. Some of the data was taken from the U.S. Census Bureau website, including *Current Population Survey.*

Population Composition – Ascribed Characteristics

In population terms, age and sex are the key characteristics that most directly influence the likely course of future population change. The key measure of sex composition is the *sex ratio* – the # of males per 100 females. It is derived from the following formula:

$$\frac{\#\text{ males in a population}}{\#\text{ females in that population}} \times 100 = \#\text{ males per 100 females}$$

Most MDCs have sex ratios of < 100 (the U.S. sex ratio is ~96.7 in 2010), while most LDCs have sex ratios of > 100. The U.S. sex ratio was > 100 until the 1940s and in then began falling; currently it seems to be rising again. Why this is so will be discussed further in class.

Age is examined in at least 3 ways – median age, dependency ratio, and population pyramids. Median age is simply the age at which half the population is younger and half is older. The U.S. median age is estimated to be 37.2 in 2010 and is rising. Many LDCs have median ages in the teens, while MDCs' median ages are typically in the late 30s.

The dependency ratio allows comparison across time and space of the age-dependency "burden" placed on a population by its dependent young and old segments. The dependency ratio itself cannot distinguish between *types* of burdens, but countries with high DRs are always LDCs with large proportions of young, while MDCs have lower DRs. Some LDCs have relatively low DRs, too, so one must be careful with analytical deductions. It is a rough, but useful measure. In the formula below, %s can be substituted for #s, as you'll be doing with your country in the first assignment. The U. S. population pyramid appears on a separate page.

$$\text{Dependency Ratio} = \frac{\# <15 + \# >64}{\#\ 15\text{-}64} \times 100 = \#\text{ dependent aged per 100 working aged}$$

Place	% < 15	% > 64	Dependency Ratio
World	26	8	51.5
MDCs	16	17	49.3
LDCs	29	6	53.8
U.S.	19	14	49.3

Place	% < 15	% > 64	Dependency Ratio
Uganda	49	2	104.1
Qatar	12	1	14.9
Russia	16	13	40.8
Italy	14	21	53.8

The Census Bureau treats race as having four groups (whites, blacks, Indians/Eskimos/Aleuts, & Asians and Pacific Islanders) and includes Hispanic Origin data *with* race, but *not* as a racial group. The U tables below for 2000(estimated) and for middle series projections for 2050 and 2100 show what happens if Hispanic Origin is included (I) or excluded (E) as a distinct racial group. I = Hispanic Origin treated just as the other 4 racial groups; E = Hispanic Origin allocated among the other 4 racial groups according to people's self-descriptions. These projections have received much media attention.

Racial Group	2000 %E	2000 %I	2050 %E	2050 %I	2100 %E	2100 %I
Whites	82.2%	71.4%	74.9%	52.8%	70.7%	40.3%
Blacks	12.8%	12.2%	14.7%	13.2%	15.0%	13.0%
Indians/Eskimos/Aleuts	0.9%	0.7%	1.1%	0.8%	1.1%	0.7%
Asians & Pacific Islanders	4.1%	3.9%	9.3%	8.9%	13.2%	12.6%
Hispanic Origin	11.8%	11.8%	24.3%	24.3%	33.3%	33.3%

Ethnicity is another complicated matter, as so many of us are of multi-ethnic backgrounds; in the 2000 census, the largest ancestral groups are German (47.8 million), Irish (34.0 million), English (28.4 million), and Italian (16.8 million). 19.7 million identified themselves as "Americans".

The above data are from the *2013 World Population Data Sheet* by the Population Reference Bureau of Washington, D.C., from the *Statistical Abstract of the United States: 2000* as referenced on an earlier page, and from the U.S. Census Bureau website.

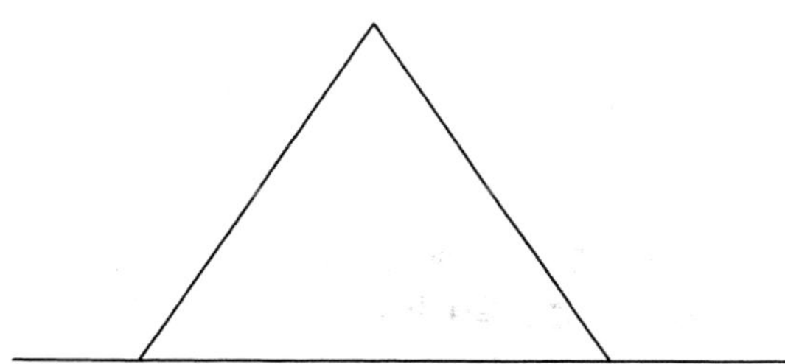

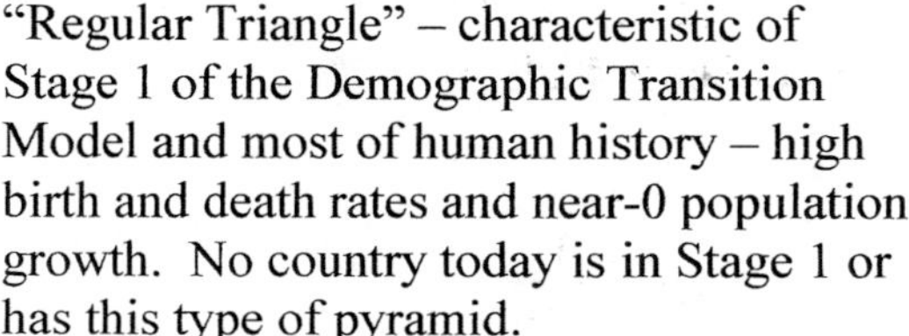

“Regular Triangle” – characteristic of Stage 1 of the Demographic Transition Model and most of human history – high birth and death rates and near-0 population growth. No country today is in Stage 1 or has this type of pyramid.

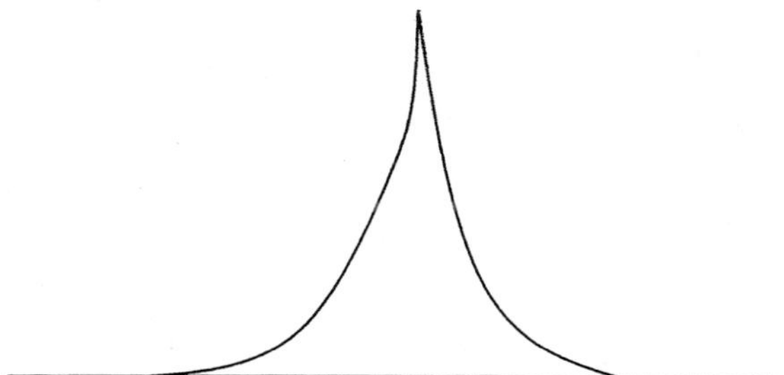

“Expansive” – characteristic of Stage 2 to mid-Stage 3 of the Demographic Transition Model – high fertility, declining to low mortality, increasing to peak population growth. Many LDCs have this type of Pyramid, which implies continued growth.

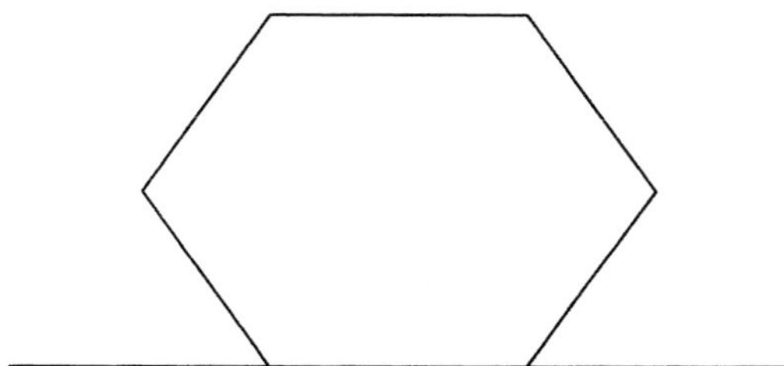

“Constrictive” – characteristic of late Stage 3 and Stage 4 of the Demographic Transition Model – declining birth rate, low death rate, and declining population growth. Some LDCs and some MDCs have this type of pyramid.

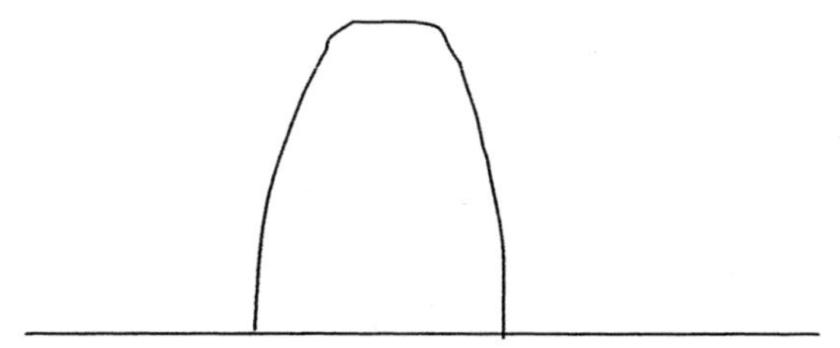

“Near Stationary” – aka “Beehive” shape - characteristic of Stage 5 of the Demographic Transition Model – low birth and death rates and near-0 population growth. Many MDCs have this age structure.

The Four General Types of Population Age-Sex Pyramids

If the MDCs that currently have natural decrease continue to do so, we may see a new type of population pyramid shape – “Contracting”. It would resemble “Near Stationary”, except that it would be pinching in at the bottom. The same might be true for world population a century from now, as world population size conceivably could shrink one day. This would also imply a new Demographic Transition Model Stage in which deaths exceeded births by a small but significant margin.

Estimated Age-Sex Population Pyramid of the United States as of 1/1/10, Based on Census Data

```
Ages                              Males                          |                  Females                          Birth Years
                                                                 |
100+                                                             |                                                   <1910
95-99                                                            |X                                                       1910-1914
90-94                                                           X|XXX                                                     1915-1919
85-89                                                        XXXX|XXXXXXXX                                                1920-1924
80-84                                                     XXXXXXX|XXXXXXXXXXX                                             1925-1929
75-79                                                  XXXXXXXXXX|XXXXXXXXXXXXX                                           1930-1934
70-74                                              XXXXXXXXXXXXXX|XXXXXXXXXXXXXXXX                                        1935-1939
65-69                                        XXXXXXXXXXXXXXXXXXXX|XXXXXXXXXXXXXXXXXXX                                     1940-1944
60-64                                 XXXXXXXXXXXXXXXXXXXXXXXXXXX|XXXXXXXXXXXXXXXXXXXXXXXXXXX                             1945-1949
55-59                            XXXXXXXXXXXXXXXXXXXXXXXXXXXXXXXX|XXXXXXXXXXXXXXXXXXXXXXXXXX XXXXXXXX                     1950-1954
50-54                       XXXXXXXXXXXXXXXXXXXXXXXXXXXXXXXXXXXXX|XXXXXXXXXXXXXXXXXXXXXXXXXXXXXXXXXX                      1955-1959
45-49                       XXXXXXXXXXXXXXXXXXXXXXXXXXXXXXXXXXXXX|XXXXXXXXXXXXXXXXXXXXXXXXXXXXXXXXXXXXXX                  1960-1964
40-44                         XXXXXXXXXXXXXXXXXXXXXXXXXXXXXXXXXXX|XXXXXXXXXXXXXXXXXXXXXXXXXXXXXXXXXXX                     1965-1969
35-39                          XXXXXXXXXXXXXXXXXXXXXXXXXXXXXXXXXX|XXXXXXXXXXXXXXXXXXXXXXXXXXXXXXXXXX                      1970-1974
30-34                           XXXXXXXXXXXXXXXXXXXXXXXXXXXXXXXXX|XXXXXXXXXXXXXXXXXXXXXXXXXXXXXXXXX                       1975-1979
25-29                        XX XXXXXXXXXXXXXXXXXXXXXXXXXXXXXXXXX|XXXXXXXXXXXXXXXXXXXXXXXXXXXXXXXXX                       1980-1984
20-24                       XXXXXXXXXXXXXXXXXXXXXXXXXXXXXXXXXXXXX|XXXXXXXXXXXXXXXXXXXXXXXXXXXXXXXXXXX                     1985-1989
15-19                       XXXXXXXXXXXXXXXXXXXXXXXXXXXXXXXXXXXXX|XXXXXXXXXXXXXXXXXXXXXXXXXXXXXXXXXXXX                    1990-1994
10-14                         XXXXXXXXXXXXXXXXXXXXXXXXXXXXXXXXXXX|XXXXXXXXXXXXXXXXXXXXXXXXXXXXXXXXXX                      1995-1999
5-9                           XXXXXXXXXXXXXXXXXXXXXXXXXXXXXXXXXXX|XXXXXXXXXXXXXXXXXXXXXXXXXXXXXXXXX                       2000-2004
<5                             XXXXXXXXXXXXXXXXXXXXXXXXXXXXXXXXXX|XXXXXXXXXXXXXXXXXXXXXXXXXXXXXXXXX                       2005-2009
              4          3          2          1          0          1          2          3          4
```

Percent of Total Population

Age Group	M %	F %	Sex Ratio	Age Group	M %	F %	Sex Ratio	Age Group	M %	F %	Sex Ratio	Age Group	M %	F %	Sex Ratio
100+	<0.1	<0.1	20.7	70-74	1.4	1.6	84.3	40-44	3.4	3.4	99.0	10-14	3.4	3.3	104.8
95-99	<0.1	0.1	28.5	65-69	1.9	2.1	88.9	35-39	3.3	3.3	99.1	5-9	3.4	3.2	104.3
90-94	0.1	0.3	41.4	60-64	2.6	2.8	92.4	30-34	3.2	3.2	100.0	0-4	3.3	3.2	104.4
85-89	0.4	0.8	54.3	55-59	3.1	3.3	93.9	25-29	3.4	3.4	101.6				
80-84	0.7	1.1	66.5	50-54	3.6	3.7	96.4	20-24	3.6	3.4	104.2				
75-79	1.0	1.3	77.0	45-49	3.6	3.7	97.5	15-19	3.7	3.5	105.3	Totals	48.9	51.1	95.7

Each bar or % represents what percentage of the total population belongs to that age-sex group; e.g., 3.4% of the U.S. population is female and ages 0-4. Or, 1.6% of the U.S. population consists of 65-69 year old males. The table shows the percentage figures depicted by the pyramid. Each age group is a birth cohort; birth cohorts generally are people who experience the same event at the same time – most typically, birth. Some pyramids are constructed using numbers instead of percentages.

These are taken from the International Data Base available on the U.S. Census Bureau's website.

United States: 1950

MALE FEMALE

Population (in millions)

Source: U.S. Census Bureau, International Data Base.

United States: 1960

MALE FEMALE

Population (in millions)

Source: U.S. Census Bureau, International Data Base.

United States: 1970

MALE FEMALE

Population (in millions)

Source: U.S. Census Bureau, International Data Base.

United States: 1980

MALE FEMALE

Population (in millions)

Source: U.S. Census Bureau, International Data Base.

United States: 1990

MALE FEMALE

Population (in millions)

Source: U.S. Census Bureau, International Data Base.

United States: 2006

MALE FEMALE

Population (in millions)

Source: U.S. Census Bureau, International Data Base.

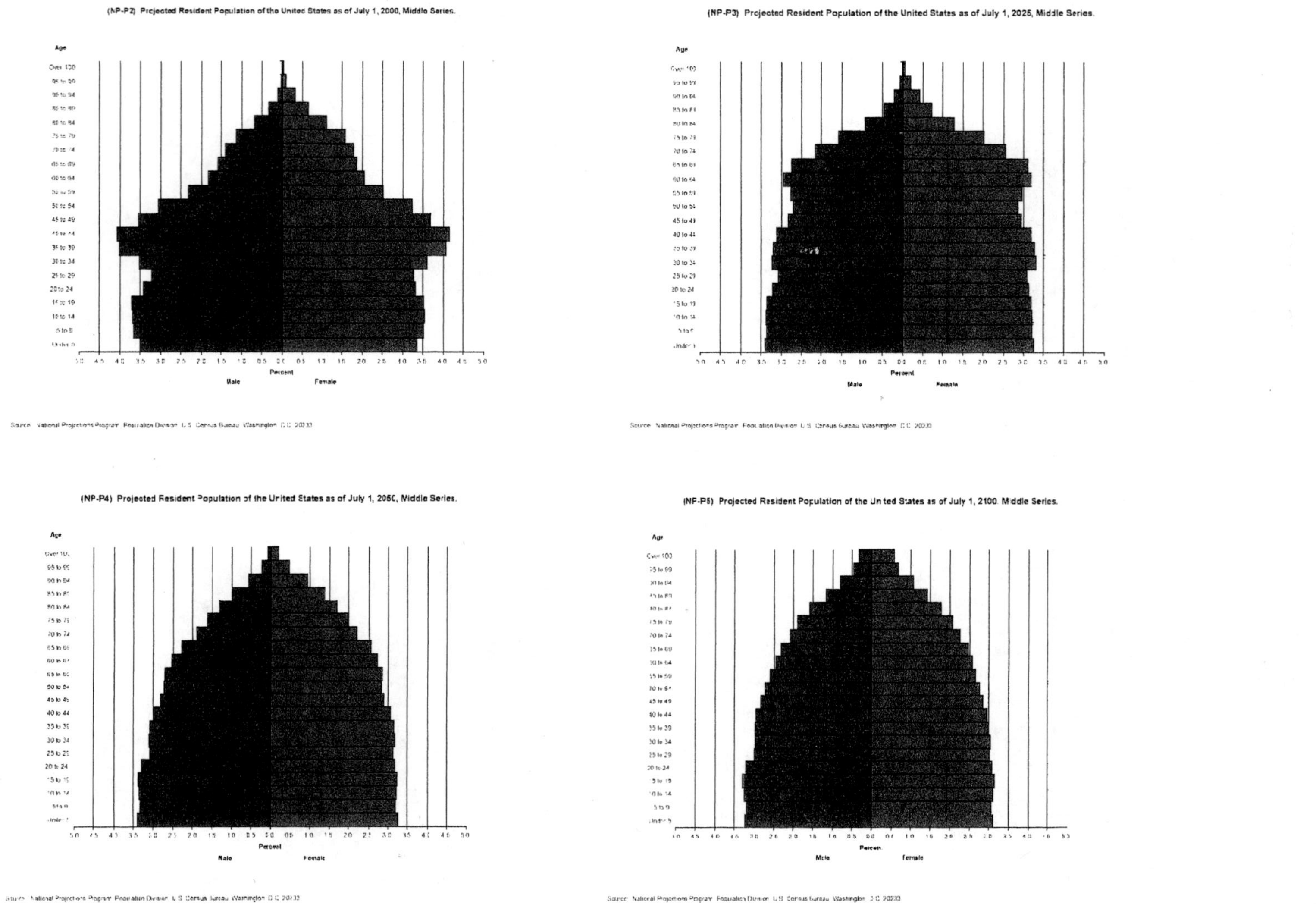

The above are the actual U.S. Population Pyramid for 2000, and the projected U.S. Population Pyramids for 2025, 2050, and 2100. Notice the changes in the shapes of the pyramids over time, particularly the loss of the bulge from the Baby Boom, and the increasingly near-stationary shape by 2100.

Mortality Outline

Data Sources, Uses & Limits
-vital registration & miscellaneous/historical sources;
-coverage/content errors

Measures of Mortality
-crude death rate & why it is "crude";
-age-specific death rates & their uses; standardization, life tables & life expectancy;
-infant mortality rate – a special case of age-specific death rates;
-neonatal /postneonatal mortality rates; early/late neonatal deaths; endogenous/exogenous causes;
-cause-specific death rates; the "epidemiological transition"; proportion dying by cause;
-maternal mortality rate, an example of rapid decline;
-morbidity measures – incidence, prevalence, case, & case-fatality rates:
incidence rate = # people per 1000 developing a disease per year;
prevalence rate = # people per 1000 having/with a disease per year;
case rate = # reported cases of a disease per 100,000 per year;
case-fatality rate = % or proportion dying of a disease of those who have it

Trends & Patterns in Mortality
-how & why mortality declined in MDCs – a matter of debate;
-differences in mortality declines in MDCs and LDCs;
-changes in the relative importance of mortality causes over time;
-"preventable"/"postponeable" deaths & life span – how long could we live?

Mortality Differentials
-how who you are affects your longevity – what are your "life chances"?
-the effects of age, sex, race/ethnicity, marital status, socio-economic status, residence;
-which are most important and how do they interact?

Points to Ponder(you may think of & raise others)
-why don't we have better mortality conditions? what could we do about it?
-should our health care system be revised? if so, how?
-should health care be rationed by age or other criteria?
-what should be the balance between preventive and curative efforts?
-does health research reflect rational decision making or political influences?
-what should be the role of MDCs in reducing mortality in LDCs?
-is reducing mortality in LDCs necessarily a good idea?
-what behaviors do you engage in that affect your longevity prospects?
-what should we do about AIDS? how much of our resources should it receive?
-should certain groups be tested for HIV? all of us? what about the right to know?
-what about real or potential environmental threats to health?
-how do we "handle" death in our culture? is there a better way?
-what should be the balance between individual rights and the greater good?
-are helmet seat belt laws, drug laws, the drinking age, etc. justifiable?
-can we reduce "extra" deaths from homicide, suicide and accidents?
-do labels matter – e.g., suicide is now "intentional self-harm"?
-are gun laws, mandatory air bags, and other regulations worth the costs?
-how much risk is "too much"? how "safe" can we be?
-how do we define "death"? what about euthanasia? "assisted suicide"?
-what would be the demographic consequences of increased longevity? how long *can* we live?
-what other mortality-related issues can you think of?

Mortality Measures

There are many measures of mortality. Of these, the Crude Death Rate (CDR) is the most commonly seen measure of mortality. Its formula is:

$$\text{Crude Death Rate (CDR)} = \frac{\text{\# deaths in a population}}{\text{average total population}} \times 1{,}000 = \text{\# deaths per 1,000 population per year}$$

For example, the crude death rate of the United States in 2010 was 8.0 deaths per 1000 population. The crude death rate is the simplest and most frequently seen measure of mortality; however, it is "crude" because it does not take age structure of the population into account. Two very dissimilar places can have identical crude death rates if one has an older population and good mortality conditions while the other has a younger population and poor mortality conditions. Except for infants and children, younger populations have fewer people in the "high risk" ages of dying; thus, a younger population's poor mortality conditions could be obscured by its age structure. Conversely, older populations have more people at "high risk" ages and that obscures its better mortality conditions. That is why mortality is typically examined by using more sophisticated measures.

These are used in several ways to get a better and more accurate picture of mortality conditions. Included among these is the Age-Specific Death Rate. In effect, it's a crude death for each age group. Its formula is:

$$\text{Age-Specific Death Rate}_{\text{zge x}} \text{ (ASDR)} = \frac{\text{\# deaths of people age x}}{\text{average total population age x}} \times 1{,}000 = \text{death rate per 1,000 people age x}$$

For example, the age-specific death rate of 21 year olds in the United States in 2006 was 0.983 deaths per 1,000 21 year olds per year. This results in a series of ASDRs, either for every age or using 5 year age groups. As this is cumbersome to use, ASDRs are typically employed as a means to several ends.

One of these ends is standardization. To compare 2 countries' mortality conditions, for example, the ASDRS of #1 could be applied to the age structure of #2; the expected deaths in #2 under #1's mortality conditions could then be determined, added, and a standardized crude death rate could be calculated. This would tell us what the crude death rate of #2 *would* be if it had the mortality conditions of #1. We could then compare this standardized crude death rate to the actual crude death rate of #2 calculated from #1's mortality conditions. Such a comparison would have the effects of the differences in age structure eliminated. We could also do the reverse to the same end – apply #2's ASDRs to #1's age structure. Since we are usually comparing more than two places at a time, we can also apply several places' ASDRs to the same standard age structure (e.g., the world's) and directly compare a set of standardized rates.

A second use is the creation of the life table (an example will be shown), often used by the insurance industry to calculate their rates. There are a few ways to construct these, but the most typical is to take a hypothetical birth cohort of 100,000 and treat it *as though* it were going to be exposed to *today's* set of ASDRs. This allows us to see how many of the 100,000 *would* survive to each age *if* today's ASDRs remained constant. In turn, the life table permits calculation of life expectancy at birth or from any age – the average # of years left. Thus, life expectancy is like doubling time in that it shows what would happen if current mortality conditions didn't change. It, too, should not be taken literally – and is one of the most frequently misunderstood demographic measures. Rather, it is a way of envisioning the future implications of current conditions should they remain constant. Although life expectancy is really just a summary measure of the present mortality conditions – and thus a period measure – many treat it as a cohort measure, one that actually reflects how long newborns or people of a certain age will really live on average. Actual average life spans for a given generation are usually longer than their life expectancies at birth would have suggested. Under 2005 conditions (ASDRs), a person age 20 could expect another 58.8 years of life on average, but most likely will average more in fact; that is, those born in 1985 will likely live to average age greater than 78.8.

The Infant Mortality Rate (IMR) is really a special ASDR for those in the first year of life. It's used as an indicator of mortality conditions specifically and standards of living generally. Its formula is:

$$\text{Infant Mortality Rate (IMR)} = \frac{\text{\# deaths to those <1 year}}{\text{total \# live births}} \times 1{,}000 = \text{\# infant deaths per 1,000 live births}$$

For example, the infant mortality rate of the U.S. in 2010 was 6.15 infant deaths per 1000 live births; in many LDCs the IMR is over 100 per 1000 live births, meaning that more than 10% of all newborns die before their first birthday. Where available data allow, the IMR can be subdivided into neonatal and postneonatal components (<28 days vs. 28 days – 1 year). The two together equal the IMR:

NMR + PNMR = IMR. In 2010, 4.05 + 2.10 = 6.15; so, most infant deaths occurred in the first month of life.

$$\text{Neonatal Mortality Rate (NMR)} = \frac{\text{\# deaths to those < 28 days}}{\text{total \# live births}} \times 1{,}000 = \text{\# neonatal deaths per 1,000 live births}$$

$$\text{Postneonatal Mortality Rate (PNMR)} = \frac{\text{\# deaths 28 days-1 year}}{\text{total \# live births}} \times 1{,}000 = \text{\# postneonatal deaths/1,000 live births}$$

Neonatal mortality can be even further subdivided into early (< 7 days) and late (7-27 days) categories where the data are very good. In 2010, the early neonatal death rate was ~3.24 and the late neonatal death rate was 0.81. Neonatal mortality is associated with "endogenous" factors, those existing before birth. These are seen as delayed fetal deaths. Postneonatal mortality is associated with "exogenous" factors – those that affect all age groups. In many ways, postneonatal is easier to reduce and is sometimes seen as an even finer measure of mortality conditions and living standards. In 2009, about half of all infant deaths took place in the first week of life – hence them being considered "delayed fetal deaths".

Cause-Specific Death Rates (CSDRs) indicate the relative importance of various mortality causes. They are used to show major causes in a particular era and allow for comparison and analysis of shifts over time. The constant 100,000 is employed for convenience. CSDRs are also used to estimate "preventable" or "postponeable" deaths. This concept relates to how much we might lower mortality; "postponeable" has become the preferred term, but the two both refer to the idea that some deaths need not take place. The formula is:

$$\text{Cause-Specific Death Rate (CSDR)} = \frac{\text{\# dying from a given cause}}{\text{total average population}} \times 100{,}000 = \text{the \# per100,000 population dying from that cause per year}$$

E.g., in 2009 11.8 people per 100,000 died in car accidents. The proportion dying from a cause can also be calculated by finding the % of all deaths due to that cause, indicating shifts over time.

The Maternal Mortality Rate (MMR) is another special case in that it focuses on childbearing women. It is somewhat like a cause-specific death rate, except that it only applies women who have given birth (since only they are at risk from this cause). It, too, is used as an indicator of mortality conditions and living standards, particularly health care quality. The MMR can drop rapidly with development and health care advances; it also plays a role in sex ratio differences between LDCs and MDCs and across time in MDCs.

The maternal mortality rate in the U.S. is just under 9 maternal deaths per 100,000 births currently – that is, for every 100,000 births, approximately 9 women die for childbirth-related reasons – or, one in 11,111. The formula is:

$$\text{Maternal Mortality Rate (MMR)} = \frac{\text{\# childbirth-related deaths}}{\text{\# total live births}} \times 100{,}000 = \text{\# maternal deaths per 100,000 births}$$

Mortality Data

1900 Death Causes – *Statistical Abstract of the United States, 1954*

Cause of Death	Rate	% of Total
Diseases of the Heart	264.3	15.4
Pneumonia/Influenza	202.3	11.8
Tuberculosis	194.4	11.3
Gastritis, Colitis, etc.	142.7	8.3
Symptoms, Senility. etc.	117.5	6.8
Renal Disease	81.0	4.7
Accidents	72.3	4.2
Malignant Neoplasms	64.0	3.7
Diseases of Early Infancy	62.6	3.6
Diptheria	40.3	2.3
All Other	477.8	27.8
Total	1,719.1	100.0

Rate = Cause-Specific Death Rate per 100,000 population.

% of Total = % of total deaths due to cause (proportion)

Note that the total is = to a Crude Death Rate of 17.2 per 1000 - similar to many LDCs today.

1900 suicide rate = 10.2
1900 homicide rate = 1.2

2010 Death Causes – *National Vital Statistics Report, Volume 61, #4, May 8, 2013*

Cause of Death	2010 Rate	2010 % of Total	Cause of Death	2010 Rate	2010 % of Total
Diseases of the Heart	193.6	24.2	Influenza/Pneumonia	16.3	2.0
Malignant Neoplasms	186.2	23.3	Intentional Self-Harm	12.4	1.6
Chronic Lower Respiratory	44.7	5.6	Septicemia	11.3	1.4
Cerebrovascular Disease	41.9	5.2	Liver (Cirrhosis, etc.)	10.3	1.3
Accidents & Adverse Effects	39.1	4.9	Hypertension	8.6	1.1
Diabetes	27.0	3.4	Parkinson's	7.1	0.9
Alzheimer's	25.1	3.1	Assault (Homicide)	6.0	0.7
Nephritis (Kidney)	22.4	2.8	All Other	137.1	17.1
			Total	799.5	100.0

2008 Leading Causes of Death for 20-24 Age Group – *NVSR, V60, No. 6, 6/6/2012*

Cause of Death	Rate for All 20-24 Year Olds	% of All Deaths	Male Rate	Male %	Female Rate	Female %	M/F Ratio
Accidents	40.6	43.2	61.7	44.4	18.2	39.0	3.4
Assault (Homicide)	15.1	16.1	25.5	18.4	4.1	8.9	6.2
Intentional Self-Harm (Suicide)	12.8	13.6	21.0	15.1	4.1	8.9	5.1
Malignant Neoplasms (Cancer)	4.6	4.9	5.6	4.0	3.6	7.8	1.6
Heart	3.3	3.5	4.5	3.2	2.1	4.5	2.1
All Other	17.6	27.7	20.6	14.8	14.1	30.5	1.5
Total	94.0	100.0	138.9	100.0	46.2	100.0	3.0

Cause of Death	White Rate	White %	Black Rate	Black %	Hispanic Rate	Hispanic %	Native Amer. Rate	Native Amer. %	Asian & Pac. Is. Rate	Asian & Pac. Is. %
Accidents	44.5	50.3	26.7	19.9	36.9	42.7	39.6	45.8	15.7	34.6
Homicide	7.8	8.8	55.4	41.5	19.5	22.5	7.5	8.7	5.4	11.9
Suicide	13.4	15.2	9.7	7.2	8.4	9.7	22.9	26.9	8.8	19.4
Cancer	4.6	5.2	5.3	3.9	5.1	5.9	3.3	3.5	5.1	11.2
Heart	2.5	2.8	7.6	5.7	2.3	2.7	2.0	2.3	2.3	5.0
All Other	15.6	17.6	29.5	22.0	14.3	16.5	11.2	12.9	8.1	17.8
Total	88.4	100.0	134.2	100.0	86.5	100.0	86.5	100.0	45.4	100.0

Examine the data; think about the patterns and comparisons. Think in terms of "postponeable" deaths, how the leading causes of death have changed, or how the causes of death among the young are unique.

Patterns of Change in Infant Mortality, 1915-2002 (*Statistical Abstracts of the United States, 1954 & 1976; NCHS Web Site, National Vital Statistics Reports, V. 58, N. 19, 5/10 and V. 61, N. 4, 5/13,* and *2006 Statistical Abstract*). All rates are per 1,000 live births per year. Note the difference over time in the relative contributions of neonatal and postneonatal mortality to infant mortality.

Rate	1915	1920	1940	1960	1980	1998	1999	2000	2010
Neonatal Mortality Rate	44.4	41.5	28.8	18.7	8.5	4.8	4.7	4.6	4.05
Postneonatal Mortality Rate	55.5	44.3	18.2	8.3	4.1	2.4	2.3	2.3	2.10
Infant Mortality Rate	99.9	85.8	47.0	26.0	12.6	7.2	7.1	6.9	6.15

Patterns of Change in White and Nonwhite Infant Mortality, 1915-2009 (*same sources as above)*

Date	White	Nonwhite	NW/W Ratio	1915-2008 Decline in # and %			
				White	Nonwhite	White	Nonwhite
1915	98.6	181.2	1.84	-----	-----	-----	-----
2008	5.3	12.6	2.38	93.3	168.6	94.3%	93.0%

The above table illustrates how the same data can be interpreted in various ways – each of which would be legitimate. In terms of absolute decline, there's a bigger drop in nonwhite than white infant mortality; in % or relative terms, the declines have been almost identical; the nonwhite/white ratio, however, is slightly worse today than in 1915. All three statements are "true", but they paint conflicting pictures of whether or not progress has been made in narrowing the racial gap in infant mortality. What do *you* think?

The racial gap in life expectancy at birth narrowed from a 13.3 year difference in 1930 to a 5.7 year difference in 1982, and was 3.8 in 2010. White females (81.3) have the longest life expectancy at birth, followed by black females (78.0), white males (76.5) and black males (71.8). 2010 data shows a 4.8 year gap between males and females (76.2 vs. 81.0). Those who are neither black nor white (Asians, Native Americans, etc.) have higher life expectancies than blacks, but lower life expectancies than whites. In the most recent data, Hispanic life expectancy passed that of non-Hispanics for the first time.

Patterns of Change in the Maternal Mortality Rate, 1920-2005 (same sources plus *National Vital Statistics Reports, V50, N15, 9/16/02*)

Date	MMR (per 100,000 births)	
1920	799.0	(similar to many LDCs today)
1940	376.0	the MMR decreased by 52.9% over 20 years
1960	37.1	the MMR decreased by 90.1% over 20 years
1980	9.2	the MMR decreased by 75.2% over 20 years
1995	7.1	the MMR decreased by 22.8% over 15 years and by 99.1% over 75 years
2010	21.0	

Note: The 1995 and 2010 data look different for three main reasons: 1) the definition of "maternal mortality" was broadened in 1999 to include some causes related to pregnancy and/or birth, 2) small changes in the numbers of maternal deaths can create larger changes in the rates, and 3) there does seem to be increasing maternal mortality It is possible that part of the increase reflects a decline in health care – the upward trend is recent and not as yet fully or satisfactorily explained.

Miscellaneous: For the curious, New Jersey is higher than the national average on heart disease, kidney disease and HIV, but lower than the national average on Alzheimer's, stroke, influenza and pneumonia, liver disease, suicide, homicide, and accidents – including motor vehicle accidents.

The sexes and races have different leading causes of death. The data below are for 2010, the last year with complete data available, and are taken from the *National Center for Health Statistics Web Page, National Vital Statistics Reports, V. 61, N. 4, 5/8/13.* All rates are Cause-Specific Death Rates per 100,000 population of the relevant group. These are not age-adjusted rates, so some of the variation among groups is due to differences in age structure. E.g., Hispanics have the youngest population, while whites have the oldest population.

Cause of Death	Non-Hispanic Whites		Non-Hispanic Blacks		Am. Indian & Alaska Native		Asian & Pac. Isl.		Hispanic	
	Rate	%	Rate	%	Rate	%	Rate	%	Rate	%
Heart	179.9	23.8	229.5	24.9	128.6	20.5	100.9	23.8	132.8	23.8
Cancer	176.5	23.4	208.8	22.7	122.4	19.7	119.7	25.7	119.7	21.4
Chronic Lower Resp.	46.6	6.2	29.6	3.2	33.8	5.4	13.9	3.3	19.6	3.5
Cerebrovascular	37.8	5.0	54.3	5.9	28.1	4.5	33.2	7.8	32.1	5.7
Accidents	42.4	5.6	32.4	3.5	46.9	7.5	15.0	3.5	25.8	4.6
Diabetes	18.2	2.4	39.6	4.3	36.4	5.8	15.5	3.7	27.1	4.9
Alzheimer's	26.4	3.5	20.9	2.3	17.2	2.7	10.9	2.6	18.5	3.3
Nephritis	13.8	1.8	30.1	3.3	16.4	2.6	9.6	2.3	14.1	2.5
Influenza/Pneumonia	14.9	2.0	17.1	1.9	15.9	2.5	14.4	3.4	13.7	2.5
Suicide	15.0	2.0	5.4	0.6	10.8	1.7	6.2	1.5	3.1	0.6
All Other	183.5	24.3	252.7	27.5	177.8	27.3	95.8	22.6	152.1	27.2
Total	755.0	100.0	920.4	100.0	628.3	100.0	424.3	100.0	558.6	100.0

The above table shows the variation among racial groups (Hispanics are treated as a fifth racial category here, as seems to be becoming more common) in terms of the ten leading causes of death in the United States. Not all of the variations are due to differences in age structure. For example, suicide is more prevalent among whites than other groups. Homicide and HIV/AIDS are actually among the 10 leading causes of death for blacks, although not for any other group or for the population as a whole. Asians and Pacific Islanders are the only group with more deaths from cancer than from heart disease, a direction in which the general population seems to be heading.

Married people have the lowest death rate (909 per 100,000 population > 15), followed by the divorced (1,678) widowed (1,678), and by the never married (1,951) – a consistent finding over time. Marriage seems to benefit men significantly more than women. Why?

The more educated also have longer life expectancies than those with less education. As you might expect, those with higher status occupations (e.g., professionals) and those with higher incomes also tend to live longer. Can you think of reasons for these findings?

Ethnicity is difficult to judge because so many of us are multi-ethnic. To the extent there are ethnic differences, in part they are genetic – e.g., Tay-Sachs disease and sickle cell anemia and in part they are due to socio-economic differences related to minority status.

Religion can influence mortality to the extent it encourages healthy lifestyles and/or discourages unhealthy ones by its beliefs and their importance. Religions that forbid smoking, for instance, would benefit their adherents.

Urban/rural residence is tricky because we now have suburbs as well, because we move among different types of places during our lifetimes, because places themselves change character over time, and because our population distribution is increasingly complex. It's an interesting case that we'll discuss in class.

Below are the ten leading cause-specific death rates by gender. These are taken from the *National Center for Health Statistics* data (Volume 61, #4, May 8, 2013) are not age-adjusted and are from 2010 data. Because more men de than women at every age, the female population is older than the male population and thus are more likely to die from chronic diseases associated with old age.

	Male		Female	
Cause of Death	Rate	% of all deaths	Rate	% of all deaths
Diseases of the Heart	202.5	24.9	184.0	23.4
Malignant Neoplasms	198.3	24.5	174.7	22.2
Chronic Lower Respiratory	43.1	5.3	46.3	5.9
Cerebrovascular Disease	39.5	4.9	49.1	6.2
Accidents	50.0	6.2	28.6	3.6
Diabetes Mellitus	23.4	2.9	21.4	2.7
Alzheimer's	16.7	2.1	37.0	4.7
Nephritis & Kidney	16.4	2.0	16.3	2.1
Influenza & Pneumonia .	15.6	1.9	16.1	2.1
Suicide	19.9	2.6	5.0	0.6
All Other	186.6	23.0	208.1	26.4
Total	812.0	100.0	787.4	100.0

The ten leading of causes of death for the sexes have both similarities and differences. Heart disease and cancer are the leading killers of both, but accidents and Alzheimer's are quite different. The differences are partly due to the discrepancy in age structure, partly due to biology, and partly due to socio-cultural factors. We cannot know definitively what the mix of biological and social roles there are in mortality differentials by gender beyond knowing that all of these contribute. We know that women enjoy some hormonal protection until menopause and we know that even after decades of women's rights battles, cultural expectations remain distinct to some degree, for example. The narrowing of the gender gap in life expectancy may indicate the influence of social change in gender roles.

The same is true for racial and ethnic differences, although in that case most believe that the bulk of the gaps in life expectancy are due to socio-economic inequities rather than biology. As discussed earlier, "race" is really a social construct, and although ethnic groups are somewhat distinctive genetically, there are relatively few and relatively minor diseases and conditions clearly traceable to genetic variations among groups. Again, after decades of the struggle over civil rights, the racial gaps in life expectancy and infant mortality have narrowed, but still exist and are still significant. Most demographers and other experts believe that most of the remaining gaps are linked to socio-economic factors. That is, if the racial groups had similar distributions on the socio-economic scale, most of those differences would disappear.

Although perhaps not a "population-related issue" in the same sense that food, resource depletion, and pollution are often discussed, mortality differentials are clearly related to remaining inequities, political issues, and social costs. In that way, these are, then, "population-related issues", just less obvious ones. Similarly, that links them to the title of this course – *Population, Resources and Environment*. "Environment" doesn't just mean the natural environment, and "resources" doesn't mean just natural resources. Even the data presented earlier pertaining to the age group of most students in this course raises many population-related issues important to our society and to us all. The differences among races, genders, et cetera have very real and important implications for public health policy and should be taken into account in policymaking. Although we can argue about degree, there is no doubt that we could reduce mortality significantly by addressing postponeable deaths, just as we have by mandating seat belts, air bags, vaccinations, and so on.

Fertility Outline

Data Sources, Uses & Limits
-registration, surveys, & historical/miscellaneous sources
-coverage & content errors

Measures of Fertility
-crude birth rate & why it is "crude"
-child-woman ratio & general fertility rate
-age-specific birth rates & total fertility rate
-what the total fertility rate really means & its relation to completed fertility rate
-replacement level fertility – meaning & expression
-replacement level fertility & its relation to zero population growth
-gross & net reproduction rates
-illegitimacy rate & ratio, aka out of wedlock rate & ratio
-abortion rate & ratio & population impact
-nuptiality – marriage rate, median age at first marriage, divorce rate, remarriage rate
-miscellaneous characteristics – birth order, birth weight, breastfeeding, C-section rates, place of birth
-expected/wanted/mistimed/unplanned births

Trends & Patterns in Fertility
-recent fertility history in the U.S. and abroad
-U.S. family composition preferences
-contraception in the U.S. and elsewhere
-the prospects for "perfect" contraception
-the fertility framework & intermediate variables – its applicability & uses

Fertility Differentials
-age, sex, religion, marital status, race/ethnicity, labor force status, socio-economic status, residence
-which are most important, how they interact & implications

Points to Ponder(you may think of and raise others)
-could there be another "baby boom"?
-does our culture *really* like children? how do we treat them?
-what are the implications of sex selection of offspring? of cloning?
-should we redefine "parenthood" and "family"? if so, how?
-what about the "problems" of illegitimacy and teen pregnancy?
-what if men bore children? how might things change?
-is there an "ideal" family in terms of size and spacing? if so, what is it?
-are older parents better, worse, or just different from younger ones?
-why are most contraceptive means designed for use by women?
-what are the social and demographic implications of the "morning after" pill?
-how much can fertility be reduced in LDCs? how much can it be "controlled"?
-how good is our system for delivering and caring for babies?
-should we have universal parental leave? universal child care?
-are children becoming a "luxury"?
-how useful are sex education and family life programs?
-do we really make fertility decisions using a cost-benefit type framework?
-how influential is birth order?
-what else can you think of?

Fertility Measures

For our purposes here, we will make a distinction between *fertility* and *fecundity*. *Fecundity* is the biological ability to produce children, while *fertility* is actual childbearing behavior. In everyday language, "fertility" is used both ways; we keep the two distinct here.

Like the crude death rate, the crude birth rate is the simplest and most often seen measure of fertility; it, too, is "crude" because it does not take into account compositional factors such as age and sex. Unlike the CDR, the CBR isn't likely to be misleading; two places with similar CBRs probably will be similar on other fertility measures. Nonetheless, it is still desirable to use more sophisticated measures in order to get a more detailed and accurate picture of fertility. The crude birth rate formula is:

$$\text{Crude Birth Rate (CBR)} = \frac{\text{\# births}}{\text{average total population}} \times 1{,}000 = \text{\# births per 1,000 population per year}$$

Another commonly seen measure is the general fertility rate (GFR). It is a refinement of the CBR in that the denominator is changed to # of childbearing age women – the population directly at risk of giving birth, as only women of a certain age can bear children. The GFR largely eliminates the effects of age and sex compositional variations, and focuses on the key group in the population that is most crucial in determining fertility. In recent years, the government has started publishing GFRs and other sex-specific measures for men; while these are sociologically interesting, they remain of secondary importance demographically. "Childbearing age" has various definitions; 15-44 is probably the most frequently used, but 10-49 is quite common and sometimes even older age groups are found. The formula for the GFR is:

$$\text{General Fertility Rate (GFR)} = \frac{\text{\# births}}{\text{\# women age 15-44}} \times 1{,}000 = \text{\# births per 1,000 women of childbearing age per year}$$

A further specification of the logic behind the GFR is the use of age-specific birth rates (ASBRs). These are much like age-specific death rates, but cover only women and only those of childbearing age. Like ASDRs, they are usually done in 5 year age groups. Although there are fewer ASBRs than ASDRs, they are still awkward to work with, especially for comparative purposes. The formula for ASBRs is:

$$\text{Age-Specific Birth Rate (ASBR)} = \frac{\text{\# births to women age y}}{\text{total \# of women age y}} \times 1{,}000 = \text{\# births per 1,000 women age y per year}$$

The way of getting around the "messiness" of ASBRs is to use them to derive the total fertility rate (TFR). If ASBRs are in 5-year age groups, each is multiplied by 5. The results are then added and divided by 1,000. The result is the TFR, the average # of children a woman *d* have *if* childbearing patterns remained constant. In this way the TFR is just like life expectancy and doubling time – it shows what ***would*** happen ***if*** things stayed exactly the same. Thus, the TFR is really a summary statistic for ASBRs characterizing present fertility patterns. Like e_0 and DT, the TFR is not intended to be taken literally.

As fertility patterns can change rather quickly, the TFR has no real relationship to actual average family size. The only way to know how many children an actual cohort of women has is to wait until their childbearing years are over – this is the completed fertility rate (CFR). For example, women born in the 1930s experienced both the "boom" and "bust" eras in their childbearing years and their completed fertility fell between the two extremes. Thus, stereotypes of the boom and bust are often exaggerated.

Replacement level fertility (RLF) is generally expressed in terms of the TFR. It is the number of children a couple must have to replace themselves in the next generation, allowing for current mortality conditions. In the U.S. and other MDCs, RLF = 2.1; in LDCs RLF is higher because mortality conditions are worse. RLF *leads* to zero population growth – after the effects of age structure have been eliminated over time; RLF and ZPG are not the same thing, however. For example, the U.S. has been under replacement level for a generation, but still has significant natural increase because of its age structure.

There are a number of fertility-related measures less commonly seen than the CBR, GFR & TFR, of which you should be aware. The gross reproduction rate (GRR) is a variation on the total fertility rate that only includes female children. It is used as another way of expressing replacement level fertility – each woman replacing herself in the next generation. Hence, replacement level fertility expressed in terms of the GRR in the U.S. would be about 1.05 daughters per woman. A still further refinement is the net reproduction rate (NRR), which is just like the GRR but with mortality already factored in. So, by definition, replacement level fertility expressed in terms of the NRR is 1.00 for all cases.

The child-woman ratio (CWR) is sometimes used where fertility data is poor or lacking, especially registration data. It divides the # of children under 5 by the number of childbearing age women times 1,000; this yields the number of children 0-4 per 1,000 women of childbearing age. It resembles the general fertility rate, except that it looks at children under 5 instead of births. The CWR in some ways is a bit better than the CBR, but distinctly inferior to the other measures. CWRs can be over 1,000 children 0-4 per 1,000 women of childbearing age where fertility is very high; by contrast, in the U.S. it has been around 300 in recent years.

The illegitimacy rate is the # of births per 1,000 unmarried women of childbearing age per year. It is calculated like the general fertility rate, but it only considers unmarried women and their childbearing behavior. The illegitimacy ratio is simply the % of all births that are to unmarried women. These are now sometimes known as the out of wedlock rate and ratio – perhaps less connotative if more cumbersome labels, reflecting changing times.

The abortion rate is the # of abortions per 1,000 women of childbearing age per year. The abortion ratio is the # of abortions per 1,000 (sometimes per 100 instead) live births per year. It gives some idea of the impact abortion has on fertility levels and thereby on natural increase, at least theoretically. Abortion data are compiled separately from both fertility and mortality data, but are usually presented with the former. Both illegitimacy and abortion vary significantly around the world and even within the U.S., as will be discussed in class.

The biological maximum is the theoretical average number of children women *could* have over their reproductive life spans. It is difficult to gauge the biological maximum precisely, since experiments would be unethical and no population allows unrestricted sexual intercourse from menarche to menopause, lacks contraception, and culturally values children very highly. The groups that come closest to approximating all of these conditions – e.g., the Amish and the Hutterites – would indicate that the biological maximum is about 12-13 children per woman, a lower figure than one might guess.

Unwanted births refer to those where a woman did not want to have any(more) children at all. Wanted births are those that were wanted at the time they occurred – the woman wanted a(nother) child and wanted it then. Between these are unplanned or mistimed (the newer term) births. These are cases where the woman wanted a(nother) child, but not at the time the birth occurred. This information is gathered by survey and generally involves retroactive interpretation of the birth – a woman is asked what her feelings were at the time the birth occurred. As many come to accept the child after its birth and/or feel inhibited about describing a child as "unwanted", more births are probably described as "wanted" than is the case in fact.

Fertility intentions are also sometimes surveyed. Women are asked how many children (or, how many more children) they *want, expect, desire,* or think *ideal.* While these words all sound close in meaning, they are intended to tap somewhat different things. Someone may think 4 is "ideal", "want" or "desire" 3 as an individual, and yet "expect" to have 2, based on her assessment of her likely future. In this way "ideal" is the most abstract or theoretical, "expect" is the most concrete and reality-grounded, and "want" and "desire" in between. You might even be able to apply these differences to your own present and foreseeable future circumstances – life is seldom ideal and we don't always get what we want.

There are numerous other aspects to fertility that will be discussed in class, with important current data provided on subsequent pages and less crucial but often interesting information given verbally. Both in an MDC such as the United States and in many LDCs, fertility can rapidly change and is a most dynamic phenomenon.

Fertility Data

Data here are from editions of the U.S. Census Bureau's *Statistical Abstract of the United States*, several of the National Center for Health Statistics' *National Vital Statistics Reports*, and from online United Nations data.

Age of Mother	1960		1975		2010	
	Rate	%	Rate	%	Rate	%
10-14	0.8	0.1	1.3	0.4	0.4	0.1
15-19	89.1	12.2	55.6	15.7	34.2	8.6
20-24	258.1	35.3	113.0	31.8	90.0	23.3
25-29	197.4	27.0	108.2	30.5	108.3	28.0
30-34	112.7	15.4	52.3	14.7	96.5	25.0
35-39	56.2	7.7	19.5	5.5	45.9	11.9
40-44	15.5	2.1	4.6	1.3	10.2	2.6
45-49	0.9	0.1	0.3	0.1	0.7	0.2
Total	730.7	100.0	354.8	100.0	386.2	100.0
	x 5 =		x 5 =		x 5 =	
TFR	3,653.5 per 1,000 women		1,774.0 per 1,000 women		1,931.0 per 1,000 women	
or	3.654 per woman		1.774 per woman		1.931 per woman	

These are the ASBRs and resultant TFRs for a near-peak baby boom year, a baby bust year, and the last year for which data are available. Note changes in rates and in the proportions of all births for each age group, especially in the key ones such as teens and older women. Also note that women who were 10-14 in 1960 were 25-29 in 1975 and just left the childbearing years in the late 1990s. Thus, they began childbearing in the boom, went through the bust and then the boomlet years. Other data for these three eras include:

Statistic	1960	1975	2010
# of births	4.258 million	3.144 million	4.000 million
CBR	23.7	14.6	13.0
GFR	118.0	66.0	64.1

Note that the number of births resembles the boom more than the bust, while the CBR, GFR, and TFR are closer to the bust than to the boom. The huge number of women from the boom era who are in their childbearing years account for this apparent discrepancy – there are a lot of them, but they are not reproducing at anywhere near the rate their mothers did. This is also reflected in the % of births by birth order below. Age structure also accounts for the fact that the TFR has been *below* replacement level since 1972 in all but a couple of years – ranging from 1.738 in 1976 to 2.120 in 2007 – yet we have consistently had natural increase. The U.S. will have to remain below replacement level for the first several decades of this century before reaching natural decrease; the further below replacement level, the sooner this will happen – but the U.S. has consistently maintained a TFR significantly higher than most other MDCs.

Birth Order	1960	2010
First	26.3%	40.1%
Second	24.6%	31.2%
Third	19.5%	16.4%
Fourth or more	29.6%	12.3%

In 2010 the U.S. had a CBR of 13.0, GFR of 64.1 and TFR of 1.931. Utah had the highest fertility of the states with 18.9, 86.8, and 2.449, respectively; New Hampshire was lowest with 9.8, 51.8, and 1.666, respectively. New Jersey was lower than the national average with a CBR of 12.2, GFR of 61.5, and TFR of 1.900.

In 2010 the sex ratio at birth was 104.8 and remains quite constant. The median birth weight has also stayed constant at 7 pounds, 6 ounces. In 2010, 8.1% of all births were low birth weight (< 5 pounds, 8 ounces), and this number is rising. In 2010 there were 34.4 multiple births per 1,000 deliveries and rising (19.3 in 1980). The proportion of twins has increased by >55% since 1980. Mean age at first birth was 25.1.

In 201`0 32.8% of all births were by Cesarean section; this represents a new peak and is more than 6 times as great as the 5% rate of 1970. In 2010 98.8% of all births were in a hospital, 0.3% in a freestanding birth center, 0.8% in a residence, and the remainder in a clinic, doctor's office or elsewhere. In 2010, 91.6% were physician attended and 8.4% midwife attended. As recently as the 1930s, most births were at home.

In 1970, only 25% of infants were breastfed; 76.9% are now – at least initially. By the age of 6 months, 47.2% are receiving some breast milk and 25.5% are still being breast fed at one year. Fecundity has remained about constant; there seem to be more fecundity problems, but also more ways of solving fecundity problems. In the early 1970s approximately 15% of births were unwanted, 44% mistimed, and 41% intended; the comparable figures in the mid-1990s were 9.1%, 21.6%, and 69.3%.

The peak months for births in 2008 were July and August, April the lowest. Tuesdays, Wednesdays and Thursdays have the most births; Sundays have the fewest, Saturdays the second fewest.

Illegitimacy Rate & Ratio (aka Out of Wedlock Rate & Ratio)

Year	Rate	Ratio
1940	7.1	3.5 (48% teens/42% 20s/10% 30s+)
1950	14.1	3.9
1960	21.6	5.3
1970	26.4	10.7
1980	29.4	18.4
1995	45.1	32.2
2010	47,6	40.8 (20.1% teens/60.3% 20s/19.6% 30s+)

Abortion Rate & Ratio

Year	Number	Rate	Ratio
1972	587,000	13.2	184
1977	1,317,000	26.4	400
1982	1,574,000	28.8	428
1987	1,559,000	27.1	405
1992	1,529,000	25.9	379
1995	1,364,000	22.9	351
2009	784,507	15.1	227

The illegitimacy ratio has increased faster than the rate, in part because legitimate births have generally declined. Also, illegitimacy is less concentrated in the 10-19 year old group than the past – note that a majority are now to women in their 20s – reflecting the fact that "teen pregnancy" and "illegitimacy" are *not* identical social issues. The ratio has been rising in other MDCs over time; LDCs vary in their emphasis on legitimacy. Values among other MDCs range from 1% in Japan and 4% in Greece to 64% in Iceland and 54% in Sweden. In 1960-64 60% of those who conceived first births before marriage got married before the birth; today only 23% do.

In 2005 Washington, D.C. had the highest rate of abortion at 54.2. New York was the highest state at 38.2; Wyoming was the lowest at 0.7. New Jersey's rate was 34.3. If all abortions in 2005 had resulted in births, the CBR would have gone from 14.1 to 18.4 and the RNI would have gone from 0.6% to 1.1%. This gives us some idea of abortion's demographic impact, albeit a maximum and not totally realistic one.

Year	Marriage Rate	Divorce Rate	Median Ages at First Marriage (male/female)	
1900	9.3	0.7	25.9	22.0
1920	12.0	1.6	24.6	21.2
1940	12.1	2.0	24.3	21.5
1960	8.5	2.2	22.8	20.3
1980	10.6	5.2	24.7	22.0
2011	6.8	3.6	28.2	26.1

Marriage and divorce rates are partially influenced by age structure, partly by cultural patterns. Alternative living arrangements are becoming more common; hence, both the marriage and the divorce rates have been declining. Median age at first marriage is higher than at any time in the last 100+ years, again largely due to cultural shifts we'll discuss in class.

Contraceptive Use & Practice

Among American women aged 15-44 in 2008, 5.4% were pregnant or postpartum, 0.4% were noncontraceptively surgically sterile, 1.7% were nonsurgically sterile, 4.1% were seeking pregnancy, and 26.6% were nonusers of contraception (19.2% had never had intercourse or had not had intercourse in the three months prior to being interviewed, while 7.4% were sexually active but not using any form of contraception). 61.8% of childbearing age women were thus surgical or nonsurgical contraceptors. The data below comes from *Advance Data From Vital and Health Statistics, Use of Contraception in the United States: 1982-2008, Series 23, Number 29, August, 2010* by William D. Mosher, et al. (Note: Bill Mosher was here at Cook as a one-year replacement in the late 1970s; I was his TA for *"PRE"* while he was here. He's been working on the *National Survey of Family Growth* and its predecessors and studying American contraceptive behavior ever since.) The data are for all childbearing age women; preferred methods vary by marital status, age, race, religion, et cetera. Although sterlixzation has grown in popularity, the increase has exclusively been among women; the same % of men have been sterilized today as in 1982.

Method	% Contraceptors Using: 1982	2008	Failure Rate
Surgically Sterile	34.1%	36.9%	<1.0%
Pill	28.0%	28.0%	8.7%
Condom	12.0%	16.2%	17.4%
Diaphragm	8.1%	n/a	14.4%
Rhythm	3.8%	1.5%	25.3%
IUD	7.2%	5.5%	4.8%
Withdrawal	2.0%	5.2%	18.4%
Implants/Injectables/Ring	0.0%	6.2%	6.7%
Other (douche, foam, wishful thinking, etc.)	4.8%	<0..1%	variable

Sterilization, the pill and the IUD are examples of "modern" (read: "more effective") methods. Worldwide, 61% of married women of childbearing age use a form of contraception, 72% of married women in MDCs and 59% of married women in LDCs. 55% of married women worldwide use modern means and 6% traditional methods. In MDCs, 62% use modern methods and 10% traditional ones. In LDCs, 54% use modern contraception and 5% use traditional means. You can compare and contrast the methods used in MDCs versus those used in LDCs, both in general and in terms of "modern" forms of contraception. You might also note the failure rates above; the failure rate is defined as the % of women using that method who become pregnant in a year. Thus, almost 1 in 5 women relying on the rhythm method will become pregnant. Although hard data on the failure rate for withdrawal is lacking, it is almost certainly quite high and comparable to rhythm and the diaphragm. The data below are from the U.N.'s *World Contraceptive Use 2007* and pertains to married women.

Method	World %	MDCs %	LDCs %
Any Method	63.1%	67.4%	62.4%
Female Sterilization	19.7	8.6	21.5
Male Sterilization	2.7	4.5	2.5
Pill	8.5	16.5	7.2
Injectable/Implant	3.4	1.0	9.4
Condom	5.7	13.9	4.4
IUD(intrauterine device)	15.5	9.4	16.5
Other modern methods	0.5	2.2	0.2
Rhythm	3.6	4.3	3.1
Withdrawal	2.9	6.8	2.3
Other traditional methods	0.5	0.2	0.6

Fertility Differentials

Rural people have more children than urban ones; this is still true in the U.S. and is generally true in both other MDCs and LDCs.

Because religion is not recorded by government agencies, religion's impact on fertility is less well know than most other differentials. One study found that Catholics' TFR was 2.3, Protestants' TFR 2.1, Jews' TFR 1.9, 1.7 for Others and 1.4 for None. Religious beliefs about contraception, abortion, et cetera, do make for differences in fertility; so, too, however do minority status and its relation to socio-economic status.

The government does now calculate equivalent measures for men as for women; e.g., the GFR and ASBRs. While these are slightly different because the numbers of men and women are different, fathers are usually slightly older than mothers, the fecundity age span is different, and so on, the patterns are similar. It still – at least for now – takes one man and one woman to produce a child (in most cases).

There's no good comprehensive data on ethnicity, partly because the combinations are virtually endless. In general, minority groups anywhere have higher fertility; much of the difference can be attributed to the relationship between minority status and socio-economic status.

Labor force participation reduces fertility – which is one reason why promoting women's rights is seen as key in reducing fertility in LDCs. In the U.S., employed women had a GFCR of 51.4 in 2006, unemployed women had a GFR of 61.2, and women not in the labor force had a GFR of 92.3.

As you have seen, the pattern of childbearing by age and how it has changed over time. Worldwide, the effect of age varies greatly from culture to culture.

In 2006, the GFR by marital status was 93.2 for currently married women with the spouse present, 58.4 for currently married women with the spouse absent, 26.2 for the widowed or divorced (mostly the latter), and 44.3 for the never married. As we've seen, marriage and childbearing are becoming de-linked in the U. S.

In general, fertility declines with socio-economic status – they're inversely related. While this is a common pattern, it is not obvious in examining the individual components of SES in the U.S., education, income and occupation. The rates below are for a given year (2010 for the first two, 2006 for the last); however, in terms of *completed* fertility over a woman's *lifetime*, the overall relationship holds up much better than the data seems to indicate.

Educational Attainment	GFR
< High School	64.8
High School	64.1
College, No Degree	55.9
Associate Degree	65.0
Bachelor's Degree	69.3
Graduate/ Professional Degree	77.2

Family Income	GFR
<$10,000	86.9
$10,000-19,999	77.4
$20,000-24,999	76.8
$25,000-29,000	61.9
$30,000-34,999	62.4
$35,000-49,999	63.9
$50,000-74,999	65.7
≥$75,000	61.5

Occupation(Women)	GFR
Operators/Laborers	38.1
Precision Production/ Repair	42.3
Farm/Forest/Fishing	69.6
Service Workers	51.0
Technical/Sales/ Administration	44.0
Manager/Professional	52.2

Religion, ethnicity, and race differences are tied to minority and socio-economic status – true in many places. If we controlled for SES, much of the racial gap would disappear (2010 data below from *National Vital Statistics Reports, V. 61, No. 1, 8/28/12*). You can make an educated guess as to who has the highest/lowest fertility levels in our society by combining characteristics.

Racial Group	CBR	GFR	TFR	% Out of Wedlock
All	13.0	64.1	1.931	40.8
Non-Hispanic White	10.9	58.7	1.791	35.9
Non-Hispanic Black	15.1	66.6	1.972	72.5
American Indian/Alaskan	11.0	48.6	1.404	65.6
Asian or Pacific Islander	14.5	59.2	1.689	17.0
Hispanic	18.7	80.2	2.350	53.4

The Fertility Framework

The "fertility framework" focuses on "intermediate variables". These are "intermediate" between social, economic and biological factors on the one hand (independent variables) and actual fertility behavior or changes in fertility behavior on the other (dependent variables). These were created by Davis and Blake in *Social structure and fertility: An analytic framework* in 1956; the immediate source here is page 98, Population: An Introduction to Concepts and Issues(Sixth Edition), by John R. Weeks, Wadsworth Publishing Company, Belmont, California: 1996.

The framework can be used to analyze current fertility behavior in one place at a given point in time, to explain fertility differences across time or place, or for policy ideas in order to try to reduce fertility. The general scheme is:

Social & Biological Factors -> Intermediate Variables -> Fertility

The intermediate variables themselves fall under three general headings relating to the three events needed to produce a birth (at least traditionally and still for most people) – intercourse, conception and gestation. Under each general heading are several specific variables.

The Intermediate Variables of Fertility

I. Intercourse Variables – those affecting exposure to intercourse
    A. Those governing the formation and dissolution of unions during the reproductive period
        1. Age of entry into sexual unions (legitimate/illegitimate)
        2. Permanent celibacy
        3. Amount of reproductive period spent after/between unions
            a. When unions are broken by divorce/separation/desertion
            b. When unions are broken by death of the husband
    B. Those governing the exposure to intercourse within unions
        4. Voluntary abstinence
        5. Involuntary abstinence (impotence, illness, separation)
        6. Coital frequency (excluding periods of abstinence)
II. Conception Variables – those affecting exposure to conception
        7. Fecundity/infecundity, as affected by involuntary causes
        8. Use or nonuse of contraception
            a. By mechanical or chemical means
            b. By other means
        9. Fecundity/infecundity, as affected by voluntary causes – e.g., sterilization
III. Gestation Variables – those affecting gestation and birth
        10. Fetal mortality from involuntary causes (miscarriage)
        11. Fetal mortality from voluntary causes (abortion)

Using these 11 variables, we can explain why the "baby boom" and "baby bust" occurred, why the U.S. has higher fertility than other MDCs, how best to attempt fertility reduction in LDCs - given their socio-economic and environmental circumstances, how socioeconomic and/or biological changes might affect fertility, and so on. For example, environmental toxins might be expected to affect #s 5, 7, and 10; if the three of these intermediate variables increased, they would exert downward pressure on fertility. One must also keep in mind the matter of strength or intensity of the variables; changes in some might outweigh opposite changes in several of the others. For example, the "sexual revolution" affected #s 1, 2, and others that would normally exert upward pressure on fertility; however, contraceptive developments (#8) and legalized abortion (#11) exerted an even stronger downward pressure on fertility. The fertility framework helps organize analysis of fertility on a more macro level in a systematic way.

Migration, Immigration, Urbanization, and Distribution Outline

Definitions & Data Sources

-definitional overlap, issues and problems;
-data sources – census/surveys/miscellaneous/immigration registration;
-legal and illegal immigration;
-coverage & content errors

Measures of Migration, Mobility, Urbanization & Distribution

-in-, out-, gross and net migration rates(one place measures);
-stream & counterstream & migration efficiency(two place measures);
-%s urban and rural; primate cities and their import;
-the metropolitan concept – how and why it evolved;
-population density – physical and nutritional/physiological variants;
-Lee's "theory of migration"

Trends & Patterns

-the major patterns of movement in the U.S.: east->west, rural->urban, city->suburb, Frostbelt->Sunbelt, metro->nonmetro, & their combined impact on our distribution;
-the geographic centers of the U.S. population & changes over time;
-urbanization & its import in the world today;
-American geographic mobility & residential preferences;
-historical types of immigration & application to today;
-worldwide population distribution;
-U.S. immigration laws & patterns, past & present – the debate goes on

Migration Differentials

-age, sex, marital status, life cycle stage, religion, race, labor force status, socio-economic status, & residence; which matter most, how they interact, and their consequences

Points to Ponder(you may think of others)

-should the events of 9/11 affect our immigration policy? If so, how?
-what should our immigration policy be - what should/can we do about/with illegal immigrants? on balance, is immigration a net plus or minus for the U.S.?
-how do we define "refugees"? how should we define them?
-is it fair to "drain brains" from LDCs and even other MDCs?
-should we have national ID cards to stop illegal immigration? would they work?
-should we register internal movements as many other MDCs do?
-should we have a population distribution policy – or is it a right to live where we want?
-what is the future of the Frostbelt, & can the Sunbelt learn anything from its experience?
-will much of the U.S. one day be a giant New Jersey? Suburbia: Heaven or Hell?
-should we simply let declining cities and small towns "die"?
-what are the effects of migration on communities, "community" and individuals?
-is local government an outdated notion? is regionalization better?
-what is/should be the relationship between cities and their suburbs?
-is the day of the single family detached dwelling over? should it be?
-what will be the effects of technology on where and how we live – when we can do most things electronically – such as school and work – will that be a blessing or a curse?

Migration, Urbanization, & Distribution Measures

Unlike mortality and fertility, migration only uses a handful of measures; all but one are interrelated. The "building blocks" are the in- and out-migration rates.

$$\text{In-Migration Rate} = \frac{\text{\# moving in}}{\text{population}} \times 1{,}000 = \text{\# in-migrants per 1,000 population per year}$$

$$\text{Out-Migration Rate} = \frac{\text{\# moving out}}{\text{population}} \times 1{,}000 = \text{\# out-migrants per 1,000 population per year}$$

These are rarely seen; however, they combine to form two more common measures.

$$\text{Gross Migration Rate} = \frac{\text{\# moving in + \# moving out}}{\text{total population}} \times 1{,}000 = \text{\# moving in and out per 1,000 population per year}$$

$$\text{Net Migration Rate} = \frac{\text{\# moving in - \# moving out}}{\text{total population}} \times 1{,}000 = \text{net \# gained or lost per 1,000 population per year}$$

The gross migration rate is the *sum* of the in- and out-migration rates; the net migration rate is the *difference* between the two. The gross migration rate is basically a measure of turnover and is useful in sociological applications. The net migration rate is by far the most used of these four measures; note that all of these pertain to individual places. There is one measure that looks at movement between two places, migration efficiency.

$$\text{Efficiency} = \frac{|(\text{moves from A to B}) - (\text{moves from B to A})|}{|(\text{moves from A to B}) + (\text{moves from B to A})|}$$

Efficiency values range from 0 (exactly equal movement between A & B) to 1 (all movement is one way). Thus, the higher the efficiency, the more one-sided movement is between the two.

Population density – sometimes called physical or arithmetic density – is often seen, but is of somewhat limited value. It is simply total population divided by total land area in square miles. It yields the average number of people per square mile, but says nothing about distribution – two places of the same density can have very different distributions, from almost even dispersal to concentration in one small area. Population divided by *arable* land area in square miles yields the **nutritional** or **physiological** density. By definition it is always greater than the more typically seen physical density above and it indicates population pressure on cropland.

Level of urbanization is usually expressed as % urban, the % of the total population found in urban areas – however "urban" is defined. In the U.S. the urban/rural cutoff is 2,500. Other places use different cutoffs. In the U.S. the urban/rural distinction has given way to that of metropolitan/nonmetropolitan, reflecting our changing distribution pattern of cities and suburbs. Since its origin circa 1950, it has been expanded and elaborated upon regularly. More on this appears later.

The median center of population divides the population into equal quadrants via a vertical line that divides the population so that half is east and half is west and a horizontal line that divides the population so that half is north and half is south. After the 2010 census the median center was in Pike County in southwestern Indiana. The mean center of population is the "balance point" so that if the country were a plane, the population would exactly balance. After the 2010 census the mean center was in Texas County, Missouri southwest of Saint Louis – the south-central part of the state. Both centers have been heading in a southwesterly direction for decades and have done so again between 1990 and 2000.

Lee's "Theory of Migration" is a sort of cost-benefit approach that is elegantly – and deceptively – simple. It has three major components – the area of origin, the area of destination, and intervening obstacles. It can be used to describe an individual's decision-making process about moving, it can be used to explain patterns of movement between types of places (e.g., people moving from cities to suburbs), or it can be used to anticipate patterns of movement. Diagrammatically, it looks something like this:

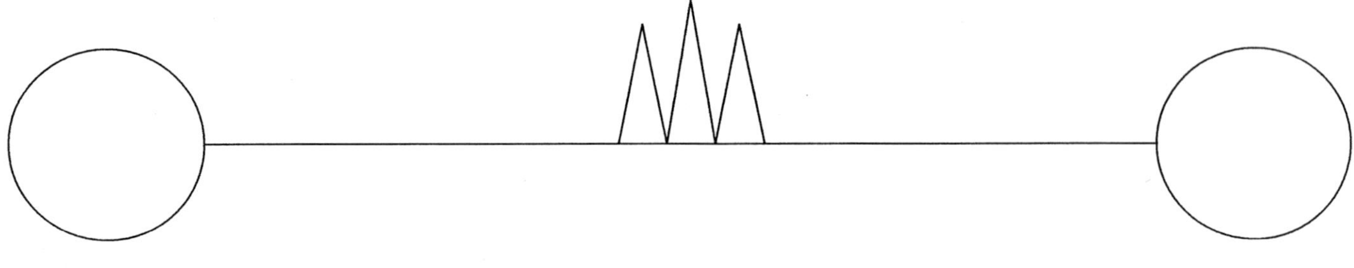

Area of Origin Intervening Obstacles Area of Destination

It's probably easiest to do an illustration of the individual's thought process. Let's say that you're living in New York – your area of origin. It has a lot of positives – diversity, culture, an almost limitless variety of activities, and so on. It also has some drawbacks – crowdedness, pollution, crime, et cetera. So the circle representing your area of origin would be a mix of +s and –s. Since it is a mix, you may think of considering someplace else to live – let's say a suburb in central New Jersey – your potential area of destination. That, too, has positives (e.g., it's greener, less overwhelming) and negatives (e.g., car dependence, less of a social scene). If the two places have a similar mix of positives and negatives, then you'll probably stay in New York.

However, if on balance the suburb has a higher ratio of positives to negatives than New York, then you might consider moving to the suburb. If the difference is small, then you'll still probably stay in New York because most of us have residential inertia – we don't tend to move easily or without good reason. If the difference is large, then maybe you would seriously consider moving.

That's where intervening obstacles come into play. In the old days, they consisted of things such as distance, effort and risk. For example, when people moved west in the 1800s, it was not a decision made lightly. There was risk of dying on the long difficult journey, it took months, it was physically challenging, and so forth. There were real physical obstacles – mountains, deserts, and weather. Today distance may be an intervening obstacle for some, but money is the biggest factor for most. So, you may want to move from New York to the suburb, but you may not be able to afford the move right now. Even if you do have the money, a fourth element, personal factors, may come into play and stop you from moving.

When we look at Lee's theory in terms of explaining patterns of movement, there are two special cases a bit different from the above scenario – "push" and "pull" migration. While many patterns can be looked at in a similar way to the individual decision-making process – because we tend to agree on the value of many features (such as crime being a negative or economic growth a positive), push and pull migration are exceptions. Sometimes people are "pushed" out of their areas of origin simply because conditions are so bad that they threaten people's survival. In some LDCs today, rural people are "pushed" out of their home rural areas because of desertification, inadequate land on which to grow enough food and similar factors. They really have little choice. Conversely, some places have such broad appeal that they "pull" people from elsewhere, even if they are not under stress and even relatively content where they are. Throughout most of the 1900s California "pulled" people from all over the United States and from other countries because it seemed a sort of paradise to many. Arguably, the United States historically has "pulled" people from all over the world; many have come to escape poverty and persecution, but many have also come simply for the opportunities and possibilities that the United States has offered.

In sum, Lee's theory can be used in a variety of ways and can be applied to our own circumstances as individuals. Think about it in terms of where you think you might like to live one day.

Migration & Distribution

The most important pattern of movement in the world today is urbanization – movement of people from rural areas to urban ones. When discussing cities, the question of the world's largest cities often arises; this is not as simple as it sounds, for there are many definitions of "city". Some use geographical boundaries and come up with smaller sizes, some use a version of the metropolitan concept and come up with larger sizes, and one currently in vogue uses urban agglomerations based on contiguous areas meeting a density criterion – also leading to larger populations. Here are three versions from the United Nations and About.com with populations in millions.

Cities		Metropolitan Areas		Urban Areas	
1. Mumbai (Bombay)	12.8	1. Tokyo	35.0	1. Tokyo	33.2
2. Karachi	11.5	2. Mexico City	18.7	2. New York	17.8
3. Delhi	11.1	3. New York	18.3	3. Sao Paulo	17.7
4. Shanghai	10.8	4. Sao Paulo	17.9	4. Seoul	17.5
5. Moscow	10.4	5. Mumbai (Bombay)	17.4	5. Mexico City	17.4
6. Sao Paulo	10.1	6. Delhi	14.1	6. Osaka	16.4
7. Seoul	9.8	7. Calcutta	13.8	7. Manila	14.8
8. Istanbul	9.6	8. Buenos Aires	13.0	8. Mumbai (Bombay)	14.4
9. Mexico City	8.6	9. Shanghai	12.8	9. Jakarta	14.3
10. Jakarta	8.4	10. Jakarta	12.3	10. Lagos	13.4

In the U.S., we use "cities" as geopolitical entities and the metropolitan area concept, which started circa 1950 and has evolved over time. With a few exceptions, the metropolitan idea uses counties as the unit of analysis. The first version basically defined a metropolitan area as one consisting of a city of 50,000 or more(or twin cities of that combined size), its county, and any surrounding counties functionally integrated with the central city in terms of commuting, density, lack of agricultural emphasis, and so on. These were called "SMSAs" – Standard Metropolitan Statistical Areas. The metro concept was born in response to suburbanization as a better way to describe our population distribution than the old "rural/urban" 2,500 cutoff point. Note that "rural", a distinct evocative image in its own right, became "nonmetropolitan" - a residual category - under the new system. Both classifications were used by demographers for the next several decades.

In the early 1980s as metro areas grew, spread, and ran into each other, the metropolitan concept was refined and elaborated upon in response to new distributional realities. Based on size, 4 categories of metropolitan areas were created and later the two largest of these were further subdivided. The largest – "Level A" – are the "supermetros" - "CMSAs"(Consolidated Metropolitan Statistical Areas) – made up of several "PMSAs" (Primary Metropolitan Statistical Areas) that were once seen as separate, independent metro areas were now blended together. Levels B, C, and D are simple "MSAs"(Metropolitan Statistical Areas), with the smallest group(D) grandfathered into continued metro status – they were metro areas under the old definition but wouldn't be today, because the total metro population is under 100,000 – another new criterion. One key factor about the entire metro concept is its dynamism; places can grow into metro status, change levels with growth (or population loss) and expand geographically as suburbs spread. The old rural/urban distinction has now largely fallen into disuse, at least in the United States. The metropolitan concept is always subject to revision.

In 2000 the Census Bureau added the concept of "micropolitan areas". These are mini-metropolitan areas in more rural settings, and are generally defined by having a central urban area of between 10,000 and 49,999 people and its county. Also similar to metropolitan areas, adjoining counties are considered to be part of a micropolitan area if they meet certain criteria that indicate functional integration with that urban center. With the addition of the micropolitan concept, metropolitan and micropolitan areas together are now called "Core-Based Statistical Areas" or "CBSAs"; so, what we once called "rural" is now "the population outside of core-based statistical areas" – even worse than "nonmetropolitan".

A few other notes as you look at the accompanying data and listen to lecture materials would include variations among "Frostbelt" and "Sunbelt" cities and among the central city/metro relationship. The older cities of the Frostbelt generally have much higher densities than the younger cities of the Sunbelt – in the 10,000 people per square mile range and "vertical" versus densities in the 3,000 per square mile range and "horizontal". Sunbelt cities are thus somewhat more suburban-like and are also more car-dependent. Exceptions include the most de-populated older cities, which have lost so many people through net outmigration that their densities are now relatively low – e.g., Detroit. Some cities make up the bulk of the metro area population (e.g., San Antonio has ~75% of its metro population), while others are in the minority in their metro area (e.g., Philadelphia has ~25% of its metro population). In many cases, especially in the Frostbelt, the central city continues to shrink in population even as its surrounding metro area continues to grow. Frostbelt cities have been hard hit by both outmigration to suburbs and to the Sunbelt region. Immigration from abroad and natural increase have only partially compensated for these losses.

Most populations that are rural are also nonmetropolitan (or, the population outside core-based statistical areas) and most that are urban are also metropolitan, but because of their different definitions these relationships don't always hold up. For example, some people in New Jersey live in small communities of less than 2,500; because <u>all</u> of New Jersey is considered metropolitan or core-based, such people would be classified as living in rural areas <u>and</u> or core-based metropolitan ones. Conversely, someone living in a small city of 5,000 in a nonmetro area would be considered urban <u>and</u> nonmetropolitan or core-based. The states show fairly disparate patterns in terms of rural/urban and metro/nonmetro distribution. For example, in 2000 New Jersey was100% metropolitan or core-based, but 94.4% urban, so 5.6% of the population lived in communities of less than 2,500. In Vermont, 73.8% of the population was core-based, but only 38.2% was urban, so the majority of Vermont's population lived in towns of less than 2,500.

Our population distribution is ever-changing and is the product of past and current patterns. One pattern has been with us since we became a country – movement from east to west. In our early days, there was always a western frontier. We are continuing to move westward, but it is now part of another pattern, that of movement from the "Frost Belt" (or, less charitably, the "Rust Belt") to the "Sun Belt". The difference now is that we are moving both west and south from the northeast and midwest – a trend that began in earnest around World War II. For several decades now, more Americans live in the south and west than in the midwest and northeast and the gap is widening. Seven of the eight states that have lost the most people to other states in this decade are Frost Belt states; all eight of the states that have gained the most population from others are Sun Belt states. .A second pattern existed at our founding and also lasted until about the time of World War II – movement from country to city or rural to urban. That pattern was superceded by another as well – suburbanization. This led to the metropolitan concept, as discussed earlier. In turn, we have come to refer to what has happened in New Jersey as "sprawl" and its attendant problems. For a time from the mid-1960s until about 1980, we had a fifth pattern – the "Rural Renaissance", or movement from metropolitan areas to nonmetropolitan ones, which also fostered sprawl. We'll discuss these patterns more in class, the reasons behind them, and the benefits and challenges they pose for us.

<u>Immigration</u>

Historically there have also been five patterns of human movement. For most of human history, we lived as hunter-gatherers and moved within relatively small areas as individuals and small groups. This has the unfortunate label of "primitive" migration. As Europeans explored and colonized the "new world", a second type emerged – "group" or "mass" movement – as people came to settle. As this proceeded and the this "new" world had significant settlement, people once again moved as individuals and families, but were not yet subject to legal restrictions; this is called "free individual" movement. Today – when we need a passport to re-enter our own country from even Canada or Mexico – we have "restricted" movement. The final type of human movement is called "forced" or "impelled" and has long existed in history. The terms are not quite synonymous, as "impelled" refers to movement that does not literally involve force, while "forced" movement is literally that. For example, many Native American groups were forced from their lands and also often forced to move to particular areas at gunpoint. Jews living in Germany in the early days of Nazi rule were not forced to leave, but as time went on it became clear to many that to stay would mean a high risk of dying – and their emigration was thus "impelled".

The U.S. has long been described as "a nation of immigrants" and "a melting pot". Despite this self-image, however, we have periodically battled over immigration, legal and illegal – often when there seems to be "too many" people coming here from places "not like us". Details will be given in lecture, but in very broad strokes, following are some key points.

Immigration increased from our founding as a nation throughout the 1800s. The composition of those coming here also changed over time. Probably the first immigrant group to bear the wrath of those already here were the Irish in the 1840s as they came to escape the famine in their homeland. Of course, today St. Patrick's Day is our biggest ethnic holiday and is celebrated by Irish and non-Irish alike (I'm sure the drinking associated with St. Patrick's Day has nothing to do with its popularity). Nonetheless, our first significant immigration laws directed at a particular group did not come along until the 1880s and were not directed at the Irish, but rather at the Chinese. Subsequent laws passed in the first two decades of the twentieth century essentially closed the door on legal immigration from all of Asia.

Immigration peaked in 1901-1910, when 8.8 million entered the U.S., for a rate of 10.4 per 1,000 population per year and contributing about 40% of our population growth. By then, the majority of those immigrants were from Southern and Eastern Europe. A series of laws passed in the 1920s aimed to reduce the number of legal immigrants overall, and were particularly aimed at the Southern and Eastern Europeans – they had "funny" names and different religions. Immigration bottomed out in the 1930s, when the total for the decade was 528,000, the rate 0.4 per year, and immigration accounted for only 6% of our total population growth in a low-growth decade. Partly this was attributable to the 1920s laws and partly to the Great Depression, which inhibited people from moving for lack of money to do so.

Since then immigration has again increased, with a range of about 600,000 to 1 million per year, a rate in the 2.9-4.0 area, and contributing about a third of total population growth. We have revisited our immigration laws almost continually since – in the 1950s during the McCarthy era, during the 1960s with Vietnam and other conflicts and social turmoil of all kinds, in the 1980s as illegal immigration came to the fore and as those coming here were increasingly from Latin America and Asia. As natural increase declines in the U.S., immigration has become an increasingly important component of population growth – accounting for about a third of our total population growth directly and contributing more indirectly via fertility of immigrants. Illegal immigration remains a hot topic and again we are debating immigration laws.

1820-2000 % Breakdown		1990s	2000s
Europe	59%	14%	15%
Asia	13%	32%	34%
Latin America	20%	48%	42%
Africa	1%	4%	7%
All Other	7%	2%	2%

"All Other" includes Canada, Australia, etc.; %s for Africa overall do not include slaves; the European % has gone up since the 90s from the break-up of the former Soviet bloc. Recently Asians have become the largest immigration group to the U.S.

The largest sending countries in this last decade have been Mexico (1,050,600), India (407,300), China (370,700), the Philippines (342,400), Viet Nam (186,100), El Salvador (173,300), Cuba (167,200), the Dominican Republic (166,000) and Korea (124,400). In order, California (1,724,790), New York (820,388), Texas (801,576), Florida (642,188), Illinois (402,257) and New Jersey (357,111) have been the largest recipient states in this decade.

The government's official estimate for undocumented immigrants in the U.S. was 5 million in 1996; this means that 5 million were here at that time, not that 5 million entered that year. This was first amended to 6 million, then new Census data put the estimate at 9 million, and later it was revised upward again to 11-12 million. In 2010, 1,042.625 people gained legal permanent resident status; 476,414 as immediate relatives of American citizens, 214,589 came under the family preference category, 148,343 under the employment preference category, and the remainder consisting of refugees, orphans, clergy, etc..

When we did population projections, we saw the quantitative impact of immigration; in the past, today, and in the future, it also has a qualitative effect as well, in that it alters our population composition. Both legal and illegal immigration have been and remain very controversial. There are numerous arguments to be made for each side of the issue, and we'll touch on them in class as well.

U.S. City & Metro Data

Top Ten U.S. Cities, 1940-2010

City	1940 Rank	1940 Pop	2010 Rank	2010 Pop	2000-2010 Change
New York	1	7,455	1	8,175	+ 2.1%
Chicago	2	3,397	3	2,696	- 6.9%
Philadelphia	3	1,931	5	1,526	+ 0.6%
Detroit	4	1,623	19	714	- 25.0%
Los Angeles	5	1,504	2	3,793	+ 2.6%
Cleveland	6	878	43	397	- 17.1%
Baltimore	7	859	23	621	- 4.6 %
Saint Louis	8	816	57	319	- 8.3%
Boston	9	771	24	618	+ 4.8%
Pittsburgh	10	671	58	306	- 8.6%
Houston	21	385	4	2,099	+ 7.5%
San Diego	43	203	8	1,307	+ 6.9%
Phoenix	148	65	5	1,446	+ 9.4%
Dallas	31	295	9	1,198	+ 0.8%
San Antonio	36	254	7	1,327	+ 16.0%
San Jose	136	68	10	946	+ 5.7%

All data is from the U.S. Census Bureau with population in 1,000s. Newark, New Jersey's largest city, was #18 in 1940 with 430,000; in 2010 it was #67, with 277,000 people (+ 1.3%). Frost Belt cities have continued to shrink or stagnate, while Sun Belt cities keep on growing. Note that St. Louis is now less than half its 1940 size, with other older cities in a like situation.

Top Ten U.S. Metropolitan Areas, 1940-2010

Metro Area	1940 Rank	1940 Pop	2010 Rank	2010 Pop	2000-2010 Change
New York	1	11,661	1	18,897	+ 3.1%
Chicago	2	4,826	3	9,461	+ 4.0%
Philadelphia	3	3,200	5	5,965	+ 3.3%
Los Angeles	4	2,916	2	12,829	+ 3.7%
Detroit	5	2,377	12	4,296	- 3.5%
Boston	6	2,178	10	4,552	+ 3.7%
Pittsburgh	7	2,083	22	2,356	- 3.1%
San Francisco	8	1,462	11	4,335	+ 5.1%
Saint Louis	9	1,432	18	2,813	- 4.2%
Cleveland	10	1,267	28	2,077	- 3.3%
Washington	12	968	7	5,582	+ 16.4%
Dallas-Fort W.	32	399	4	6,372	+ 23.4%
Houston	20	529	6	5,947	+ 26.1%
Atlanta	21	518	9	5,269	+ 24.0%
Miami	51	268	8	5,565	+ 11.1%

In contrast to the cities, all of the metro areas continue to have population growth, except Pittsburgh and Cleveland. By comparing the above table with this one, it is clear that central cities are small components of their metro areas and older metro areas have held up better than their central cities. As we'll discuss in class, the metropolitan concept is a complex and fluid one.

Classification	Population	2000-2010 % Change	% Total Population
Core Based Statistical Area (total)	289,261,315	10.3	93.7
Metropolitan Areas	258,317,763	10.8	83.7
Micropolitan Areas	30,943,552	5.9	10.0
Outside CBSAs	19,484,223	1.8	6.5

In 2010, the U.S. was thus 83.7% metropolitan (about two thirds in suburbs and one third in central cities) and 16.7% were nonmetropolitan. NJ is considered 100% metropolitan, with 11.6% in central cities, 88.4% in suburbs and 0% nonmetropolitan. In 2000 the U.S. was 79% urban and 21% rural, while NJ was 94.4% urban and 5.6% rural – this distinction has all but disappeared now.

Mobility & Migration Differentials

The following data is from the *2012Statistical Abstract of the United States*, from *Geographic Mobility – Population Characteristics, March 1999 to March 2000*, issued in May, 2001 as part of the U.S. Census Bureau's *Current Population Reports* series, and from C*urrent Population Reports, April, 2009.* From 2009 to 2010, 87% of Americans did not change residence and were thus "nonmovers". Of the 13% who did move, 9% moved within the same county, 2% moved to a different county within the same state, and 1% moved to a different state. The overall percentage of movers is down from about 20%; it had seemingly leveled off at about the 16% mark, but now has declined further. Local moves are more likely to be for housing/neighborhood related reasons, longer ones more likely for job-related or family reasons. Overall, 43.7% of moves were for housing reasons, 30.3% for family reasons, 16.4% for job reasons, and the remaining 9.6% for other reasons.

Among the regions of the U.S., in 2008 the South gained 253,000 net migrants at the expense of each of the other 3 regions, while the Northeast had a net loss of 123,000, losing to the South and West and gaining some from the Midwest. The Midwest lost 97,000, with net in-migration from the West and net out-migration to the South and Northeast. The West lost 43,000 more migrants to the Midwest and South than it gained from the Northeast. This is a departure from the more typical pattern of recent years in which both the South and West gained at the expense of the Midwest and Northeast. Politically this is important because Congressional reapportionment is taking place; New Jersey is losing a seat while states such as Arizona gain seats.

Age: Young adults are the most likely to move; contrary to popular belief, the elderly are the least likely to do so. Following is the breakdown by age. Can you think of explanations for this pattern?

20-24	27% movers	1-4	20% movers	30-44	14% movers	10-14	11% movers	65	3% movers
25-29	26	5-9	14	15-19	12	45-64	7		

Sex: 12.1% of males moved, while 11.1% of females did. Males are more likely to make longer moves, females shorter ones, though their overall rates are similar.

Race: 11.1% of whites moved, 15.6% of blacks, 13.1% of Asians, and 17.0% of other races. Formerly, whites made more long distance moves than others, but that no longer seems the case. Asians and Hispanics are relatively mobile because they are our two largest immigrant groups.

Marital Status: 7.7% of those married with spouse present moved, 19.2% of those married with spouse absent, 5.1% of the widowed, 13.9% of the divorced, 22.3% of the separated, and 17.6% of the never married.

Socioeconomic Status: 22.8% of those below poverty level moved, 16.3% of those with 100-149% of poverty level income, and 9.7% of those with ≥150% of poverty level income. 15.8% of those with incomes of <$25,000 moved, 13.7% of those with $25,000-$50,000 income, 9.4% of those with $50,000-$100,000 incomes, and 6.6% of those with incomes of >$100,000. Education's pattern is more varied – 11.6% of those with < high school moved, 9.4% of high school graduates, 11.1% of those with some college, 9.8% of those with bachelor's, and 9.3% of those with a graduate degree. Mobility used to be more directly correlated to socioeconomic status; now they have an inverse relationship.

Religion: Lacking data, there seems to be no significant direct relationship between major religions and mobility. For some (e.g., the Amish), mobility is likely less than that of larger, more mainstream groups.

Ethnicity: Ethnicity is complicated, as we have discussed. There seems no direct correlation between ethnicity and mobility except in rare cases and/or to the extent it is related to socioeconomic status.

Labor Force Status: Couples in which both partners work have lower rates of mobility than those in which only one works. As a practical matter, this should not be surprising.

Population Issues & Policy

As we return to examine the population-related issues most people think of first – economic development, resources, environmental impact and food, we also return to the population perspectives and how each sees these issues. At this point, a few remarks on the evolution of population thought are in order.

For most of human history (99%+) population growth was negligible and not visible to people because they lived lives limited in geographic scope and exposure to much beyond their immediate environment. They lived short lives and lacked our means of communication, so population was a non-issue.

As time went on, population growth accelerated slowly and gradually people (at least some of them) started to, live longer lives and see a bit more of the world. Eventually population growth did become noticeable. When it was recognized and for centuries after, to the extent it was recognized it was seen as a good thing. At a technological level where people fought with spears, bows and arrows, et cetera, "in numbers there was strength" – particularly in terms of numbers of young adult males. Later a second reason was added – population growth was seen as an indicator of economic growth and prosperity.

Although a few observers did not see population growth as a good thing, it was the Reverend Malthus who popularized the view on an ongoing basis in the late 1700s and early 1800s (hence the term "Neomalthusians"). Malthus was disturbed by the poverty around him in England, particularly the poor houses where many lived in horrible conditions. In thinking about this issue, Malthus was drawn to the conclusion that the fundamental reason was too many people. He believed that population increased exponentially (1, 2, 4, 8, 16, etc.), while the "means of subsistence" (i.e., food) could only grow arithmetically (1, 2, 3, 4, 5, etc.). He looked at land, labor, technology and capital and saw that land would be a limiting factor – as the population grew and people used more land to grow food, "the law of diminishing returns" came into play. That is, the new land put under cultivation would be of lower and lower quality so that it would produce less than the land already in production.

In considering the possibilities Malthus saw two general options, what he called "preventive checks" and "positive checks". There were two sub-types of "preventive checks" – "moral restraint" and "vices". Either alone or together could keep fertility and thereby population growth under control. "moral restraint" was Malthus's preferred route and consisted of no pre-marital or extra-marital sex, not getting married until one could afford to, and not having children unless one could afford them. "Vices" consisted of prostitution, homosexuality, contraception and abortion. While these could limit fertility and population growth, Malthus opposed these on moral grounds. If the "preventive checks" did not keep population growth under control, then the (unfortunately named) "positive checks" would come into play – war, disease, famine, and plague. These would increase mortality, thus keeping population in balance with the means of subsistence. Malthus's view was not entirely original, but his perspective has endured since his time – waxing and waning in popularity with the state of the world.

The disasters Malthus anticipated did not occur, largely because he underestimated advances in technology, especially in agriculture and industrialization. Marx came along later in the 1800s and called Malthus a "plagiarist" (which was not true) and the "gloomy parson", among other things. Although there had been many advances between Malthus and Marx even as population growth accelerated, poverty was still common and Marx offered a very different explanation for its existence – relations among the "haves" and "have nots". For Marx poverty was the result of inequitable distribution. The world offered enough to provide an adequate standard of living for all, even with further population growth. For Marx the concept of "overpopulation" was an example of "false consciousness" – a smokescreen issue that capitalists hid behind and that allowed them to blame the victims for their own plight. Marx thought this concept obscured what he saw as the real problem – a capitalist economic system and its concomitant social system. Revolution was thus his answer. Like Malthus, his ideas and view of population's role (or, non-role) in world problems have endured.

More recently the "High Tech" view has evolved. In this perspective, taking the long view of human history, we see progress accompanying population growth. 200 years ago we had less than a billion people on the planet; today we have more than six times that amount and the majority of today's population has a higher standard of living – often much, much higher –than almost all of those alive then. Some High Techs believe that population growth is a good thing – it spurs us on, it means the birth of more Einsteins, and so on – while others may not necessarily see it quite that way, they do agree that it is not a negative.

"Deep Ecologists" or "Greens" are an even more recent arrival. In the United States we have groups such as Earth First!, in Europe there are Green political parties with this viewpoint. Popular concern with the environment is relatively new, so it's not surprising that this perspective is, too. The notion that we should act on the presumption that the planet comes before our species is still a foreign concept to most.

Moderates have probably been around as long as there has been recognition that population size and growth might affect us. Moderates often lean toward one side or the other of the Neomalthusian to Marxist/High Tech ends of the spectrum. In the United States – to the extent people have thought about it at all – most Americans would probably describe their views under this heading.

Population & Economic Development

Generally there is an inverse relationship between rate of natural increase and gross measures of economic affluence. For example, we can look at the Population Reference Bureau's *2013 World Population Data Sheet* and observe:

Place	RNI (%)	GNI PPP($)	Place	RNI (%)	GNI PPP($)
World	1.2	$ 11,690	United States	0.5	$ 50,610
MDCs	0.1	$ 35,800	Liberia	3.3	$ 600
LDCs	1.4	$ 6,600	Switzerland	0.2	$ 54,870

(GNI/PPP = Gross National Income in Purchasing Power Parity per capita – the amount of goods and services one could buy in the U. S. per person.)

Clearly the above illustrates the point that places with low RNIs have high GNI PPPs and that those with high RNIs have low GNI PPPs. There are exceptions to this rule. Former Soviet bloc countries are relatively low on both (e.g., Ukraine at -0.3% and $7,290). Oil producers are relatively high on both (e.g., Oman at 1.8 and $25,580) – although this doesn't take into account distributional inequities. Nonetheless, the general relationship holds true and the key question about it is one of *causality.*

Neomalthusians argue that more population growth means a lower standard of living. Thus, LDCs must reduce population growth in order to improve the standard of living – cutting population growth is necessary for economic growth. They hold that population growth reduces investment capital, spreads gains thinly across the population, produces diseconomies of scale, consumes resources needed for development, creates unemployment, and increases socioeconomic stratification. They point the ever-widening gap between MDCs and most LDCs as evidence. Some even suggest that there are LDCs with no real prospects for much economic development – places with too many people and too few resources to *ever* rise above impoverished status. For Neomalthusians, the fact that MDCs have an RNI of 0.2% and a GNI/PPP of $35,800, while LDCs have an RNI of 1.4% and a GNI/PPP of $6,600 and Least Developed Countries have an RNI of 2.5% and a GNI/PPP of $1,430 is proof that population growth restricts economic development. For Neomalthusians, population growth must come down for the standard of living to rise. Similarly, they link the fact that about half of the world population lives on $2 per day or less to high fertility.

In contrast, Marxists and High Techs argue that population growth is no hindrance to economic progress and perhaps stimulate it. They claim that population growth means a better quality labor force (as younger, better educated workers replace older, less educated ones), produces economies of scale, prods economic/technological improvements, and provides larger markets for products. Some even argue that with more births, the number of geniuses in the world rises – who can then contribute to invention and innovation. In their eyes, economic development (and/or redistribution in the case of Marxists) must occur and the standard of living must rise in order for population growth to come down. They point to the history of MDCs and those LDCs that have seen economic growth as evidence for their view. They claim that people will reduce fertility and thereby the RNI when they feel economically secure and have faith that their lives and their children's lives will continue to improve. They would interpret the MDC-LDC RNI-GNI/PPP relationship as meaning that economic growth and an improved standard of living must be fostered in LDCs in order to reduce the RNI. While these two views are in general agreement, they would clearly differ in terms of relative emphasis on growth versus redistribution – both within individual nations and internationally. Both believe, however, that all countries can achieve an acceptable standard of living. Unlike Neomalthusians, there are no countries they would consign to permanent poverty.

Moderates would see the need to attempt to improve the standard of living and reduce population growth simultaneously, because they view the two as being mutually influential. Many observers envision a future wherein a handful of countries (e.g., the U.S.) will comprise a small economic elite, a second tier of countries will be developed industrially to a fairly high level (e.g., many former Soviet bloc countries), followed by a third group of former LDCs who will attain a modestly successful standard of living (e.g., India), and a fourth group that will be in dire straits (e.g., some African LDCs) and prone to military and political conflict. At the same time, it is difficult to imagine the day when most of today's LDCs will not be "*less* developed" than today's MDCs. It is, perhaps, somewhat easier to envision a day when all countries might be able to adequately meet the basic needs of their citizens.

Deep Ecologists would have a drastically different take on the population-economics issue. They might agree with the Neomalthusians that population growth must come down – likely agreeing with the more extreme Neomalthusians that ultimately population size must decrease. They would also agree with some Marxists that the emphasis on economic growth is misplaced – some already have "too much", and their excess could/should be redistributed to those with "not enough". However, most Marxists are not opposed to further economic growth, while many Deep Ecologists see little need to pursue "more"; indeed, many would advocate reversion to a simpler lifestyle with fewer "things". Clearly, Deep Ecologists would have little in common with the High Techs.

While it often seems easiest to agree with the Moderate view, policies usually must choose between them to some extent – at least in emphasis. The disagreement between the extremes boils down to the contrast between the following:

Neomalthusian: ⇓Population Growth ⇒ ⇑Standard of Living

versus

Marxist/High Tech: ⇑Standard of Living ⇒ ⇓Population Growth

See what you think of this real life example:

Country	CBR/CDR/RNI			IMR/LEB/Child Mortality			TFR/Contraception		GNI/PPP
"A"	15	6	0.9	21	74	5	1.8	80/77	$ 11,720
"B"	17	6	1.2	12	74	2	2.1	68/53	$ 6,120

Demographically the two countries are very similar even though Country A is far more affluent – how might you explain this? We'll cover it in class.

Population & Resources

The Neomalthusian view of resources is sometimes described as the "Limits Thesis" (e.g.,by Ridker and Cecelski in the Population Reference Bureau's Population Bulletin *Resources, Environment, and Population: The Nature of Future Limits*, Vol. 34, No. 3, August, 1979). It is based on the following:

1) there are limits to population and economic growth imposed by the earth;
2) those limits are near;
3) as we approach those limits, death rates will soar;
4) *even if* the limits are further away than we suppose, population growth and economic development ought to stop in the name of future generations and in the name of LDCs.

The view at the other end of the spectrum – the High Techs and Marxists – is sometimes described as the "Cornucopian" view. It is based on the following:

1) there are only limits on resources if science and technology cease growing;
2) this is not likely – and technology "creates" resources;
3) *even if* there are no further scientific/technological advances, the earth is huge relative to the demands placed upon it, and population growth and economic development can continue for a long time.

A moderate viewpoint might incorporate elements of each of the others; e.g., agreeing with the Limits view that the earth is finite in terms of resources, but disagreeing that resource limits are imminent. A moderate might also advocate economic growth for the foreseeable future – a la the Marxist/High Tech view – but still want to see population growth reduced. There are other possible interpretations as well.

Deep Ecologists have another attitude toward resources altogether. While the other perspectives focus on having enough resources for the population and confine their debates to how to accomplish that end (technology, population growth reduction, redistribution), Deep Ecologists question the right of humans to consume resources to begin with. With their preservation ethic, the point for them is to consume as little as possible; neither economic nor population growth is desirable - in fact, both should be minimized.

Limits people use current resource problems as evidence for their position – deforestation, desertification, looming oil and mineral shortages, and so on. They emphasize *known* reserves of resources presently being used – supplies of existing resources that we *know* are out there and that we can obtain with existing technology at an affordable cost. They make statements such as "at current rates of consumption, oil reserves will be depleted by the year 2040"; they tend to assume that we will not or cannot change. They view resources – at least some nonrenewable ones – as fixed in quantity. Hence, they also subscribe to the concept of "carrying capacity" – the number of people that that planet can support on an ongoing basis. Some argue that we may have passed that point already (e.g., the organization Negative Population Growth, a more extreme group than the better-known Zero Population Growth group).

Cornucopians cite history as evidence – humans have moved from whale oil to coal to petroleum to nuclear energy forms, all the while raising the standard of living. History for them is the story of human progress – more people live at higher levels of wealth than ever before. New technologies allow us to use things we couldn't use before; thus, we create resources technologically. They talk in terms of *prospective* reserves – quantities of existing resources we *think* are out there and will *become* attainable at a reasonable cost in the future with new technologies. They also talk in terms of *resources* generally – anticipating that things we currently can't use will become useful to us. "Resources" really are just things that we are both capable of using and willing to use; they thus have both technological and socio-cultural components. High Tech Cornucopians assume that we will always be able to invent our way out of resource problems.

Moderates usually blend these views in some fashion and advocate a mix of strategies – conservation, renewable resources, recycling, improved efficiency, redistribution, new technologies and socio-cultural change – in order to keep resources and population in balance. Deep Ecologists might favor some of these as well, especially less consumption and more conservation, renewable energy sources, efficiency, recycling and redistribution. For them the point is to consume as little as possible. On this issue one question to consider is how much difference lowering population growth would make, especially given ever-rising levels of consumption in MDCs and the desire for greater consumption in LDCs. Even if population growth slowed or ceased, would resources still be a problem? To what extent? Would everyone then be able to have "enough"?

One other idea worth noting is the "population resource region". This concept distinguishes among world regions by taking into account population, technology and resource availability. There are four types. Much of Europe is high consumption, high technology, but also has a high population/resource ratio. The U.S. and a few others are in the best position – high consumption, high technology and a low population/resource ratio. Some LDCs have low consumption, low technology, and a low population/resource ratio – and therefore at least have potential for development. Many LDCs, however, are in the worst position – low consumption, low technology, and a high population/resource ratio. This group is in a poor position to aspire to greater consumption and face the most risk of permanent LDC status. This is one reason why some observers believe that some LDCs may never have the ability to develop economically.

Population & Environment

The Ehrlich-Commoner debate, carried on over some years by these two and their allies, summarizes the disagreement over the population/environment relationship. It began with Ehrlich's equation $I = P \times F(P)$, where I is total environmental impact, P is population, and F is environmental impact per person. He argued that as P increases, F does, too. Thus, population has a "double whammy" effect on the environment, affecting the environmental both *directly* through growing numbers and *indirectly* by increasing the amount of impact per person as well. One example he gave was the case of houses being built around a lake. Each new house means more impact on the lake, but at various points each new house has a disproportionate impact. First, a sensitive fish species might be lost. In turn, this will have a series of further ecological consequences – another fish species that was previously prey might now flourish at the expense of other species, and so on. After a series of such events and with continued construction of houses, Ehrlich argued, a "tipping point" might be reached and the lake could "die" in any meaningful ecological sense. Therefore, population was the key to environmental health. With such illustrations, Ehrlich was a major force in resurrecting population growth as an environmental issue in the 1960s.

Commoner revised Ehrlich's equation, subdividing his F(P) component into two separate parts – what he labeled affluence and technology. You may be familiar with the revised "IPAT" equation (some use "C" for consumption instead of affluence): $I = P \times A \times T$, where I is again total environmental impact, P is again population, A is affluence in terms of consumption per person, and T is technology in terms of impact per unit of production. It is further assumed that consumption and production are functionally equal, so that the units appropriately cancel out. Commoner argued that T was the crucial factor in the equation; population and affluence change rather slowly and incrementally, while technology changes quickly and in quantum leaps. Commoner examined a number of pollutants and how they increased after World War II, his most famous example being beer. He argued that the American population didn't increase much in the 25 years or so after the war and that affluence didn't change much in terms of beer consumption per person; therefore, the culprit was technology in the form of disposable containers holding the beer consumed. With returnable containers making a comeback in many states and recycling being employed in others, the environmental impact of beer subsequently has been reduced. What is needed, then, is socially-controlled applications of technology to minimize environmental damage. The same sort of argument might be made about cars – the kinds of cars we drive may be more important than how many of us are driving or how many cars we have. Commoner is making a Marxist-type argument here, claiming that the O->T relationship in the POET scheme is the most crucial. Ehrlich would see P->E and P->T->E as most important, with O having little direct role.

High Techs would argue that to the extent technology creates environmental problems technology can also fix them. There is little need, then, to worry about social control of technology's effects. For example, industrial technologies generated unprecedented environmental impacts on water and air; once that was recognized, new technologies were created to alleviate these problems – e.g., smokestack "scrubbers" or oil-eating bacteria. In the end, technology need not harm the environment significantly; some might even argue that technology can make a "better" environment. Indeed, some would argue that the environment is "better" today than it was 100 or 200 years ago. While the car pollutes, we forget that the horse did, too.

Moderates might see the inevitability of increasing environmental impact with increasing population size; that is, the more people, the more impact on the environment – Ehrlich's "direct" effect. However, they might well also recognize the need to regulate new technologies – e.g., cloning – and to promote environmentally friendly and remedial technologies as well. They would also be likely to recognize the need for or desirability of socio-cultural changes to reduce impacts – getting away from the "throw away" mentality, perhaps promoting high density housing and/or mass transit instead of suburbia and the car, mandating recycling, and so on. The precise mix of approaches taken from the other views is appealing at first glance, but also tricky in terms of being successful.

Deep Ecologists might agree with the Moderates in recognizing that population, affluence and technology all have impacts on the environmental and that all three need to be addressed. Where they would disagree is in terms of the severity of the impact each of the three has and the resultant need for more far-reaching policies than Moderates would be willing to advocate. The Deep Ecologists see the environment as far more threatened than Moderates do and therefore see the need for stronger remedies.

It may be hard to imagine a cessation of population growth in the immediate future and/or equally difficult to imagine a world in which material progress is voluntarily halted. If so, then to the extent one is concerned about pollution/environmental impacts, the burden might be seen to rest on technology and on socio-cultural changes whereby new technologies are created and introduced in a more conscious manner, not simply applied because we can do something new. In addition, socio-cultural change might work toward creating new definitions of "affluence" and conditions under which population growth could be reduced. As with other population-related issues, environmental impact quickly becomes thorny, and the difference between what "can" be done versus what "will" be done is particularly crucial. You might consider the Gulf oil spill in terms of these views.

Population & Food

When most people think of population-related issues, the first thing that comes to mind is food. While there are some common areas of agreement among "experts" on the population/food relationship, there are also many areas of disagreement. Most would agree that there is enough food in the world today to adequately nourish the world population and would also agree that the fact that there are hundreds of millions who are malnourished is the product of uneven distribution. Beyond this, the picture is largely a matter of the facts chosen to emphasize. There is no objective "truth and beauty" view all can agree with here. For example, a few years ago the United Nations Food and Agriculture Organization put out two reports in a matter of months that came to rather opposite conclusions. One chose to emphasize that the *proportion* of the world population that is malnourished has been decreasing, that calories per capita have been increasing despite population growth, that China and India are now largely self-sufficient, that some LDCs who were formerly food importers are now net food exporters, that there is no reason to suppose that food production technologies – agricultural and otherwise – will cease progressing, and so on. The other report focused on such facts as the *numbers* of malnourished people have been increasing, the rate of nutritional improvement has been declining, that food reserves and arable land per capita have been decreasing, that the MDC/LDC food gap remains and perhaps is widening, that the Green Revolution has run out of "easy tricks", and so forth. The reports had different authors, but that they came from the same well-respected international agency speaks volumes about the controversy and lack of certainty involved.

Optimistic observers tend to focus on long-term trends – gains made over the last 30-40 years. In this light, the population/food relationship has improved. Pessimists tend to look at short-term trends, the last 5-10 years; in many areas during this time period, the population/food relationship has either stopped improving or has lost ground. Whether short-term trends are simply fluctuations in a long-term pattern of progress or the harbingers of a difficult future, no one can know for certain. The FAO once calculated that the planet *could* support 33 billion people – three times as many as moderate projections suggest world population size to be when zero population growth occurs – *if* everything were done correctly. Others have gone as high as 50 billion in what Neomalthusians call "carrying capacity". Some Neomalthusians, on the other hand, would suggest that we have already exceeded carrying capacity as a practical matter – and that world population size will have to decrease soon, quite possibly through increased death rates.

Neomalthusians argue, among other things, that many of the agricultural techniques we have used to cope with population growth in the short term will subvert food production in the long term - pesticides and fertilizers will ruin land and water, overgrazing causes desertification, and so on. Hardin's "lifeboat ethic" and the Paddock brothers' "triage" schemes claim that we should be prepared for the day when some LDCs will, in effect, have to be written off in terms of food aid and allowed to "die" so that others will make through the "time of famines". More "optimistic" Neomalthusians say there's a little time left to achieve ZPG, but not much; otherwise, Malthus' "misery" or "positive checks" will restore the population/food balance for us. Even this group suggests we are nearing the day of reckoning.

High Techs are confident that breakthroughs in biotechnology and similar areas will allow us to provide more and better food for more and more people. They point to the Green Revolution's accomplishments and anticipate more of the same. Whatever unpleasant side effects were produced by the Green Revolution can be fixed and the lessons applied to the future. Negative unintended consequences are, in their eyes, less serious than starvation and malnutrition.

Marxists have varying degrees of faith in technology, but virtually all include improved distribution as part of their solution. They share with the High Techs a faith in our ability to produce enough for the growing world population, while suggesting that addressing inequities will necessarily play some role in feeding people adequately. Many Marxists believe that cash crops put many LDCs in a "no-win" situation, for example. Crops such as coffee are common enough so that prices LDCs receive for their coffee crops will never be sufficient for them to either purchase enough food or to purchase the means to produce enough for themselves. Debts to coffee importers keep them producing coffee for the cash to pay enough on their debts to remain marginally economically viable – a vicious cycle.

Moderates want to attempt to reduce population and maintain/improve food production simultaneously. Which they emphasize more depends on whether they fall on the Neomalthusian side or the High Tech/Marxist side of the population continuum; few are precisely in the middle. They usually favor what they see as more "practical" solutions – more family planning programs, selective use of new agricultural technologies, more conservation of land and water resources, and so on. Neomalthusians might see this as "too little, too late", while Marxist/High Tech types might not see all of these as necessary.

Deep Ecologists want to see population growth halted about as badly as Neomalthusians, are generally not big believers in or advocates of technological solutions, and are concerned with distribution in the sense that they often favor eating lower on the food chain – plants instead of animals – to improve efficiency of food consumption and to lessen environmental harm. What Deep Ecologists advocate might be seen by most others as lowering the standard of living in terms of food and more generally as well. They often seem to emphasize the environment's concerns over people's concerns.

There is a myriad of potential solutions to the population/food problem. Improved storage and transportation in many LDCs would help a great deal and are relatively easy in the sense that all they cost is money and they are not controversial, do not require change, and are do-able now. Technology may hold great promise, but it produces unintended consequences and cannot be counted upon. Redistribution and reduced waste and vegetarianism at the individual and institutional levels can be done, but are generally unlikely to be done. Population growth is coming down, but it is not clear that it is decreasing fast enough, nor is it clear that fertility and thereby population growth can be "controlled" in any meaningful sense. In the population/food relationship, many of the things that *could* be done are unlikely to be done and many of the things that are most likely to be done won't make that much difference. Think about some policy alternatives and see if you don't find this to be the case. If time allows, we'll do this collectively in class.

Population Policy

Many government policies affect population growth, often unintentionally. During the baby boom, for example, it was suggested that the income tax deduction encouraged people to have children; that is, it was "pro-natalist". If that were ever true, it surely isn't today; no one has children in modern America in order to save tax money; instead we have a "marriage penalty" in the tax system that presumably has an "anti-natalist" effect. Congress has debated ways to reduce or eliminate this penalty; should that happen, it's certainly questionable as to whether or not it would have the effect of increasing American fertility. More typically, however, we think of population policies in terms of reducing population growth by lowering fertility. With some notable exceptions, such as China, the primary means of reducing population growth has been Family Planning Programs (FPPs). It should also be noted that some countries may have renewed interest in pursuing policies that *raise* fertility – MDCs with natural decrease and/or an aging population with too few young workers, for instance.

FPPs' stated aim is to give people the knowledge and means to have the number of children they want when they want them. While fertility and population growth have fallen in the last several decades, the question is whether FPPs will be sufficient to bring the world population to ZPG "in time". They have been criticized on many grounds – the absence of goals, the failure to attain goals in the rare cases where they have existed, the fact that many people *want* 4, 5, or 6 children, the inability to overcome cultural norms and prohibitions, the absence of abortion in many FPPs, and generally being insufficient. The severity of criticism depends on the import one ascribes to population as a cause of world problems.

Some years ago demographer Bernard Berelson came up with 6 criteria by which to judge FPPs and potential alternatives: technological availability, administrative feasibility, economic feasibility, political feasibility, moral/ethical considerations, and presumed effectiveness. His conclusion was that on balance, FPPs were the best of a bad lot. Again, the easiest things to do generally have the least effect, while the things that would have the greatest impact are the most difficult to implement. Alternatives such as mass sterilants were very effective, but low on political and moral/ethical grounds. Raising the marriage age might be acceptable on the first five criteria, but would not have a tremendous effect on fertility unless set very high and unless illegitimacy were also taboo. Financial incentives are unfeasible in poor countries, and so on. FPPs have had the greatest impact where economic development has occurred and people are motivated to use them. When introduced in a vacuum, they have tended to have less effect.

The 1994 World Population Conference started moving away from FPPs as the primary hope for reducing fertility for the first time. They emphasized women's empowerment – greater rights, education, employment, et cetera, as a new and better approach. To the extent this succeeded, women would presumably be motivated to take advantage of FPPs and be able to do so. Women's roles are still controversial in our society, much less in many traditional cultures. However, to the extent women's rights movements in the U.S. and other MDCs have changed women's roles, fertility declines have generally followed. Recall the fertility framework and the baby bust to envision how this scenario can play out. It is too soon to tell how well this new approach will work.

People often speak of "population control". That would seem to be a misnomer. China has tried more things to reduce fertility and to end their population growth than any other country – and yet their population growth is far from "controlled". They have reduced their fertility and rate of natural increase, but ZPG is not yet in sight. Further, many of the methods they have employed would be unacceptable on a variety of Berelson's criteria in a more democratic society. If China has been unable to reach ZPG yet, it seems the prospects for other high growth countries are not great.

India has the longest standing attempt to reduce population growth via FPPs and related programs more acceptable to democratic societies. Here, too, the results are not the most encouraging. India is lagging behind China and is expected to pass China in population in the early part of the next century. When goals have been set in India, they have not been met. At one point a too-zealous program offering incentives such as transistor radios for vasectomies became a political issue that led to the downfall of the government. After 50 years of FPPs in India, it still has considerable population growth and relatively high fertility.

The 1994 World Population Conference set a goal of ZPG at 7 billion people. After taking this course, you should have some appreciation for just how ambitious that goal is. We passed the 6 billion mark last year and we have been adding another billion every dozen years or so. Thus, this goal means bringing population growth to something of a screeching halt. Recent trends have been encouraging in terms of direction - both world fertility and rate of natural increase have been dropping, as we discussed earlier in the semester (see data below). Speed, however, is another matter. If we look at the rate of decline of world population growth or world total fertility rate, the pace is similar to that assumed by demographers' moderate projections – replacement level fertility would be reached in mid-century and ZPG at the end of the next century, leaving us with a world population in the 10-12 billion range. This is clearly a far cry from 7 billion. The following data illustrate change in the approximate life span of a college senior's lifetime. The direction of change may be encouraging, though the speed of change is obviously unsatisfactory to many. See what you think.

Level	1978 Population/CBR/CDR/RNI/TFR		2013 Population/CBR/CDR/RNI/TFR	
MDCs	1.173 billion	16/ 9/0.7%/2.0	1.246 billion	11/10/0.1%/1.6
LDCs	3.148 billion	33/12/2.1%/4.4	5.814 billion	22/ 7/1.4%/2.6
World	4.321 billion	29/12/1.7%/3.8	7.137 billion	20/ 8/1.2%/2.5

Data are from the 1978 & 2013 editions of *The World Population Data Sheet*, Population Reference Bureau.

From *World Resources 1996-97 – A Guide to the Global Environment*, World Resources Institute, et al and *The 2013 World Population Data Sheet:*

Country	1950 Population	1970-5 CBR/CDR/RNI/TFR	2013 Population	CBR/CDR/RNI/TFR
China	555 million	28.3/ 6.3/2.2%/4.8	1.357 billion	12/ 7/0.5%/1.5
India	358 million	38.2/15.8/2.3%/5.4	1.276 billion	22/ 7/1.5%/2.4

As the world's two largest countries that comprise about one third of the world population, it is clear that both have a ways to go before reaching ZPG. In most respects, China has made greater and faster progress than India and is closer to stabilizing its population size. In fact, most demographers expect India's population to surpass China's by mid-century. China's "one-child" policy is onerous by our standards, while India's approach has generally been more democratic – if less successful. Contraceptive use among married women of childbearing age in China is 87%, virtually all modern means. In India, after more than 50 years of family planning efforts, 56% use contraception, 49% modern means and 7% traditional means. Can we have an effective fertility reduction policy that is effective *and* democratic? Some countries have, but each country's circumstances are different. Can India? Could China if its political form was less rigid? It's difficult to know.

No population perspective wants to see population reduced via increased death rates, but they do disagree on the importance of population in world problems, how imperative it is to reduce world population growth, and what the best and most appropriate means of accomplishing that goal are. As people of knowledge and sincerity disagree on these issues, you are certainly entitled to have your own opinions about them. For Neomalthusians, population is essentially the root of all evil; they have been wrong before, but need only be right once to be vindicated. High Techs have an abiding faith in human ingenuity and note that we have faced and largely conquered problems before, but that doesn't mean we will always be able to do so. Marxists believe in the perfectability of human institutions and relationships; theoretically this may be true, but we haven't seen this capacity in fact. Deep Ecologists believe that we should put the environment first and learn to live within its means, but in dealing with all of our other problems this view has not taken hold as other priorities seem more important. Moderates may seem at first glance the most reasonable, but run the risk of error should either side of the spectrum be proven correct, ultimately. Whatever your perspective, and regardless of whether or not it has changed after taking this course, you should be aware of the spectrum of thought about population and appreciate the complexities it entails.

End Note

I hope that you have enjoyed the course. I also hope that you will not fall prey to the numerous population "myths" out there that we have discussed throughout the semester, that you have a better appreciation for the complexity of population studies and for the role of population in the world today and in your own life, that you have some new concepts and understanding that will prove useful to you in the future, and that you will take away some interesting questions to ponder periodically in the years ahead, personally and professionally. If the preceding goals have been accomplished, then we have had a successful semester.

As I complete this edition in June of 2014, the U.S. Census Bureau's "population clocks" show a world population of 7,176,146,234 and the American population at 318,251,157. Both the world population and the U.S. population have more than doubled in my lifetime – and I'm not *that* old. We presume and hope that your generation will live longer than mine, but we don't expect the world population to double again in your lifetime – and most of us hope it won't. The American population may or may not do so. In any case, both *will* continue to grow and change for quite some time – and you will have to deal with the effects of that growth and change. I hope you and your generation are a bit better equipped to do so than mine.

GFC